EASY AS PB&J

Share what you know.
Make money doing it.

Tamsen & Chris Horton

ISBN: 978-0-9979348-0-9

Cover Design: Perry Elisabeth Design | perryelisabethdesign.com

Editing: Ronei Harden | roneiharden.com

Authors' photo courtesy of Tamsen & Chris Horton

Advance Praise

Easy As PB&J works! Everyone has a PB&J inside them! Without hesitation, I recommend this system to anyone who is looking to create a new online course, an informational product, a book, or simply needs clarity about what they should create. Being able to work directly with Tamsen on two different PB&J products in my business, besides being a seamless process, I loved the collaboration. Being able to work with her to bring out the BEST of my ideas was a win-win-win! I'll never make another product or service without using the ideas and systems of Easy As PB&J.

Holly Gillen, Go-To-Video Gal | hollygstudios.com

Easy As PB&J ROCKS!!! I'm going to have my husband read it he's ready for some PB&J! Anyone who needs a boost of motivation to get going on their dreams and see how SIMPLE sharing what you know and making money doing it needs to read this book. Simplicity rather than overwhelming is the ONE thing that I'd say is the most important thing to know about Easy As PB&J.

Elyse Sparkes, fitness professional | elysesparkes.com

You can do it! Do it scared! *Easy As PB&J* is perfect for anybody that is looking to live a different life; a life of freedom. I LOVE how relatable it is. We all have a story and talent to share and *Easy As PB&J* shows you how to do it!

Jenny Taylor, Entrepreneur | shedoesgrace.com

This book will change so many lives! Tamsen and Chris are an inspiration, this book comes from their hearts and their desire for people to live independently and happy. ANYONE can share what they know and make money doing it and it really is as easy as making a peanut butter and jelly sandwich. I know so many smart women who have so much to offer but feel stuck in their box. *Easy As PB&J* would open so many doors for them! For myself, reading it was inspiring and I have so many ideas that will help me create a niche for myself as an attorney.

Samantha Meza, Attorney | sjflaw.net

I think the most important thing to know about *Easy As PB&J* is to keep an open mind. You may not be able to use these ideas RIGHT now in life but the information will stick with you until you have your own "AHA" moment and when you do you'll have the knowledge at your fingertips. After reading *Easy As PB&J*, I was so inspired and wanted to jump up and DO something! I felt fully capable of accomplishing my own PB&J.

Agata Lefere, Pediatric Dentist | grandvillepediatricdentistry.com

"*Easy As PB&J* is brilliant! It is a game changer as it opens up possibilities you never knew existed. I wouldn't change a thing and would recommend it to everyone I know because it opens up possibilities and gets people thinking in a brand new way. It addresses the mindset necessary--as well as the tools--to share your gifts with the world."
Deana Welch, Energy Advisor | deanawelch.com

"The most important thing you have to know about *Easy As PB&J* is it is simple, effective, and fun. Before using this system I was scattered and unfocused. The PB&J system helped me to focus on the customer experience and customer needs when creating my products."
Cheyne Scott, Attorney & Mindfulness Coach | thespirituallitigator.com

"I recommend *Easy As PB&J* for anyone looking to add "more" to their life. The conversational tone, practicality and encouragement offered throughout the book was truly enjoyable."
Busy Professional

"*Easy As PB&J* is ideal for anyone wondering how else to create income with what they know and I definitely recommend reading it. I really enjoyed the personal stories and the PB&J formula of how to create a product based on something you love."
Busy Professional

"Above all *Easy as PB&J* is a simple system to create and market tangible products creating multiple streams of income. Thank you for making the process easy to understand. Other systems require complicated software or hundreds of dollars. This is a system ANYONE can implement."
Ronei Harden, Editor | roneiharden.com

"The most important thing you need to know about the PB&J system is it's super simple and quick and it's stinking genius! Before using the PB&J Course Design system I was spinning my wheels. The six-week program to help business owners create a website that works - the idea that came out of my first run through of PB&J Course Design went on to create over $24,000 in income through its BETA launch. If you asked me if I'd keep using the PB&J method to create my next product my answer is -- Abso-freakin-LUTEly! Crystal clarity and ideas with substance have been emerging like wildfire. There's no stemming this tide."
Laura Husson, Founder and Director at Husson Media Ltd | laurahusson.com

Dedication

For Bo, forever and always the hero of our hearts and
the daily inspiration that fuels our dreams.

Table of Contents

Game Changing Thank You

Chris: Peanut butter and jelly sandwiches were my "go to" school lunch as a kid, gently packed into the latest and greatest character lunch box just waiting for me.

No matter what happened earlier in the school day, when lunch time came around, opening my lunch box and finding a PB&J was always a little sprinkle of joy in my day. I can honestly say strawberry jam and smooth peanut butter is as good as it gets served on plain white bread, of course.

Fast forward nearly thirty years, and the comfort and joy of peanut butter and jelly once again weaves its way back into my life.

PB&J renews so many perspectives, as childhood memories often do, reviving emotions that seemed tucked away underneath years of "adulthood". Now and then, you need a reminder to live the life you truly love once again. I have to thank my wife, Tamsen, for bringing PB&J back into my life in such a sweet way.

When you meet her, you'll agree...she is simply amazing. Of course, I am supposed to feel that way and say nice things about her. Only Tamsen could take the simple idea of making a peanut butter and jelly sandwich and relate it to packaging and selling an idea. She has the superpower of demystifying the complex concept. Time after time, I hear friends and clients comment on her ability to simplify the world and do so in a calming way.

Lucky fella indeed...

Tamsen always tests out new ideas and problem solving strategies with Yours Truly as the guinea pig. I knew she had something pretty cool brewing when I overheard her talking about PB&J Course Design™ with her online friends.

Secretly, I started thinking, "What if I made a course?" This was completely different for me. I'd always accepted myself as simply focusing on one thing when it came to my occupation - I am a teacher. Period. The end. Giving myself permission to think I could do more was scary, intimidating, and automatically shut me down as my self-protection walls went up - the unknown is uncomfortable.

Despite my limiting beliefs, I allowed myself the freedom to quietly think. *What is one part of teaching that I absolutely love?* I created a list of my favorite teaching moments that truly inspire joy in my life. When I do these specific things during the school year, I am in my zone of genius. My soul begins to light up thinking "What if?"

What if I could take the parts of my day I really love and expand them to be a larger part of my day? Powerful stuff, right?

One day while driving home from the gym, I decided to share one of my ideas with Tamsen. I knew full well by sharing my interest with her, she would grab my hand and allow me to run with it.

You must understand—when Tamsen sees the faintest glimmer of awesome on the horizon, she is all about making it shine as bright as it possibly can. She wants the best for anyone and everyone, genuine to the core.

An hour later, I sat down on one of our Adirondack chairs on our screened-in porch, while Tamsen set up shop in her office on her computer. She set up the session for us to video chat through the PB&J process and off we went. Initially, I was battling nerves and other feelings of uncertainty.

As only Tamsen can do, she broke down all those walls within minutes and I was in her place of creative genius. My original idea quickly blossomed into a flood of new sparks that turned into many amazing avenues in which to share my joy with others in a helpful format. The crazy and surprising part was how much fun we were having. It was like the chains of limitation were breaking apart, one after another. I was becoming creatively free. I FINALLY saw the power Tamsen's skills can provide others. After thirty-seven minutes, my PB&J course was complete and I was hooked! I wanted more. I saw how much I had to offer, and I wanted to keep digging for more gold!

Since that enlightening summer morning, I feel like a new person. Motivated, encouraged, and empowered. Just like when I opened up that lunch box when I was an elementary school kid. The day was brighter and everything was a little sunnier.

PB&J course creation opened my eyes to view the world differently and to see the missed opportunities that have been right there all along. To think PB&J is simply a course creation journey is limited in thought and why we needed to write this book for you.

I can honestly say, yes, it created an idea and a course, but it also provides an opportunity to slow down your day to a point where you can enjoy the moments in life that were meant to be enjoyed. Hearing my kids laugh, being silly with them, feeling a calm breeze, and being present in that moment—these things are happening all the time, but for the first time in a long time, I am now able to appreciate the *now*.

I encourage you to be bold enough to take your own PB&J journey. Get back what's most important to you.

Thank you to my wife, Tamsen. Thank you for our marriage, our two beautiful boys, and most importantly, thank you for believing in me.

Time to open up the cupboards, get out your peanut butter, bread, and jelly. Be bold.

Allow yourself this freedom; it's awesome. Let your creative journey begin.

INTRODUCTION

"Can you remember who you were, before the world told you who you should be?"
Danielle LaPorte

Chris & Tamsen: Imagine taking the expertise you've spent your lifetime accumulating and transforming far beyond what you are currently doing for "work". Reigniting the excitement of your hobbies, passions, and profession by creating additional income streams to fuel your soul and your checking account.

Has your childhood of sandboxes, blanket forts, and tea parties far too quickly turned into an uncomfortable chair stuck in a room with only a clock to look at? That can stop today.

You played by the rules, finished college, got a good job, got married, and had a couple of kids; now you're finding you want more. But more what? Time? Money? Freedom?

Are you unwilling, as we were, to wait until age sixty-five for your "more" to show up?

Ahead lies an adventure we'd like to take alongside you, and it's as easy as making a peanut butter and jelly sandwich.

Who are we to write this book?

Well, we're a lawyer (Tamsen) and a teacher (Chris), parents to Kip and Tad who simply had a nugget (one could say a "peanut") of courage to quietly ask, "What if?"

What if we could have "more" now?

What if we could remove the limitations imposed by our professions and find other ways to share what we know and make money doing it?

Well, we did exactly that and now we want to share not only our stories but also our step-by-step system, *Easy As PB&J*, with you.

Please join us on this adventure. We will walk with you every step of the way to show you how you can use what you already have—your knowledge, skills, hobbies, passions, areas of excitement or expertise—and expand your income, your freedom, and the choices available to you throughout your life starting today.

How would having *extra* income impact your family? What if you could create that extra income simply by taking what is already in your brain and learning how to turn it into an ATM?

Easy As PB&J is the quiet whisper to encourage you to see that no matter what you are currently doing to earn income, you have opportunities inside you that combined with a new perspective, clear instructions, and built-in cheerleaders, you can change your life.

As Steven Spielberg said:

> *[W]hen you have a dream, it doesn't often come at you screaming in your face, "This is who you are, this is what you must be for the rest of your life." Sometimes a dream almost whispers. And I've always said to my kids, the hardest thing to listen to—your instincts, your human personal intuition—always whispers; it never shouts. And if you can listen to the whisper, and if it tickles your heart, and it's something you think you want to do for the rest of your life, then that is going to be what you do for the rest of your life, and we will benefit from everything you do.*

Listen to the whispers as you turn each page. This is our wish for you right now.

Why did we write this book?

We're not single, twenty-somethings, who can focus 100% on growing the next great Internet sensation of a company. We're forty-something parents of two amazing kids, student loans, professional degrees, mini-van driving, real life people who simply want you to know 1000% that if you want "more" you can have more without leaving what you already love and worked hard to achieve behind.

To think that you're simply a [occupation] limits you. You are the totality of all your —life experiences, sports played, instruments learned, and obstacles overcome—and so are we. We simply learned how to cash in on the totality of who we are while still keeping our [occupations] and so can you!

We want you to know that you already have everything inside you that you need to take your life where you want to go - *to live doing what you love surrounded by the people you love.*

Who is this book for?

It's for you.

It's for each of our friends. Amazing, brilliant, inspired, loving, caring individuals who deserve to have the opportunity to wake up each morning excited about the day that lies ahead. To spend as much time with the people that they love and have the money to support all the "more" that they want to fill their lives with.

It's for every single person who has worked to play by the established rules of education and professions and is feeling like they were sold an empty bill of goods.

For parents whose hearts break just thinking about going back to work when their new baby is weeks old, but they feel they have no other choice.

For servicewomen and men who gave their hearts, minds, and souls to keeping our family safe; and are now retiring wondering what do they do next?

For families facing terminal illnesses, who want to quit everything and enjoy every single deliciously sweet moment they have together, and can't because they need to pay the bills and that means they have to spend the best hours of their days at "work".

For the billions of professionals who are sitting on goldmines and don't even know it.

For families whose investment accounts and retirement plans are sources of stress instead of daily celebration.

For college students who thought they knew what they wanted but now are questioning whether the "established" system is going to work for them.

For school-age kids (*and really that's all we are - lifelong learners*) who have ideas and whose parents are smart enough to know they don't have to wait until they graduate college to share what they are excited about and make money doing it NOW!

For home builders, flooring installers, home painters, and thousands of other trades who can equip and empower a whole new generation of HGTV® addicts; and divorce themselves from continually trading their time and labor for money.

For newlyweds who want to intentionally design a life they love and want to live each day on their terms.

For parents who want to capture normal everyday moments on Tuesday mornings, or Thursday afternoons with their kids without worrying about losing their jobs, missing school, or anything else. To know that they have the security to do what they *know* is best for their family, *when it's right for their family.*

For retirees with generations of wise life-experiences and professional knowledge, who can create an additional income stream where they never knew one was possible.

Eliminating stress over whether the government programs will take care of them and what happened on the stock market last night.

For the "professionals" who love yoga, traveling, canning vegetables, painting, or _____ and simply need a little nudge that they CAN create income streams from those passions.

We wrote this book for you and the unique talents and skills you have to offer to the world.

How to use this book?

The first time through we recommend reading it through in the order we've presented it. We want to make sure you see how the peanut butter, the jelly, and the bread fit together. After you've read through once, then you can come back to it and go straight to the section you want to work on.

We recommend using a journal to record your thoughts and ideas as you go through this book and definitely encourage writing in the margins, drawing pictures, and using lots of sticky notes! The multimedia experience is your companion digital workbook and also contains downloads for the exercises that you can use. (bit.ly/pbjmultimedia)

What is PB&J?

Easy As PB&J is the book version of the ideas and systems that are taught in our PB&J Course Design™ online training. PB&J Course Design is a digital product that Tamsen created to share what she knows with the world (business, legal, creativity, and organization) and make money doing it.

PB&J = the sandwich and represents the digital product you can make to sell by packaging the areas of excitement and expertise you already have into pieces of content.

P = the peanut butter represents "Personality." All the pieces of *you* that are essential to creating the PB&J product that's right for you. This is the gooey deliciousness inside you of who you want to be and how you want to feel each moment you are living life.

B = the bread represents your "Buyers." The people you will share your areas of excitement or expertise with while they pay you for the value you've added to their life.

J = the jelly represents your "Joy" and is the specific area of your excitement or expertise that you want to package and sell to people.

Here's what you can expect from reading this book.

You don't need to quit your current job, change jobs, jump off a cliff, buy expensive anything, sign up to earn pennies on the dollar on the latest social media get-rich-quick scheme, or anything else that would fall into a high-risk or just plain stupid category. All you need to do is open up your mind to the possibility of a new perspective.

Ultimately, the process of learning how to take what you know, share it with others, and make money doing it will take you on your own personal journey. You'll learn how to identify the unique areas of expertise and excitement within you and how to take what is in all respects "mushy brain stuff" and step-by-step create a digital product that produces solid income.

The short-version of the *Easy As PB&J* journey we'd like to share with you goes something like this:

First, you're going through life carrying the ingrained thoughts that have brainwashed you into believing that you are ONLY what you do - "I'm a [occupation]*.

That's all I do. Period. The end. I go to work, do my thing, and money shows up every two weeks in my checking account. No more, no less."

Then, you start reading this book and start to quietly wonder: "Yes, I'm a [occupation]*, but I'm starting to understand *how I could* make and sell a digital product that would expand my income beyond what I'm currently doing for 'work'."

Finally, you'll reach the last few pages and realize that you've taken on a new perspective and belief system: "Yes, I'm a [occupation] but *that's only one part* of me. *Easy As PB&J* showed me how to take what I already knew and create a way to expand my income streams beyond my 'traditional' job. Now I see opportunities for creating PB&J products all around me--my love of couponing, my mad skills about kayaking the Colorado River ... "

We know this journey well. We've both gone through the life-changing PB&J process and we'll never go back to being "just" our jobs. We don't have to and now you don't have to either.

There're a few other terms you'll see us mention throughout this book and we want you to know what they mean.

#hometeam = The friends and family you consider your "family." You'll hear us talking about your home team throughout the book because *Easy As PB&J* is a team affair.

#vacationinglife = A mindset to create a life where you feel like you're always on vacation. Spending your time surrounded by people and experiences that leave you feeling full of joy.

PB&J Course Design™ = An online training program that helps individuals take what they know and create their own digital product in under an hour that they can sell to twenty people** for $100 each month after month.

Snack Time = Exercises designed to help you take action. While each can stand on its own within this book, most have additional information available in the multimedia experience. *We simply couldn't put the videos in the book!* (bit.ly/pbjmultimedia)

You're going to see the entire PB&J Course Design system; however, if you *simply can't wait* to get to "the system" then skip on ahead (keep in mind you're going to miss some really good ingredients that will make your PB&J extra good!)

* lawyer, dentist, artist, gym teacher, kayak enthusiast, hair stylist, horse trainer, crafter, yard-sale guru, accountant, smoothie bar owner, butcher, baker, cake decorator ... simply insert your occupation.

**The twenty people for $100 each month after month is a starting point and used to keep the focus on creating the digital product and not becoming bogged down with the math. PB&J Course Design™ is used by individuals all over the world creating digital products from FREE to multiple thousands of dollars.

You've Got This!

Have any of these thoughts *popped up* in your mind?

"I'm just an [occupation], I don't need to do anything else. I don't want to do anything else but I'd really like to make more money."

"Sure, technically I know a lot of "stuff", but not really anything that's special to me. A hundred other people know what I know and honestly, no one is going to pay me to tell them what I know because they can look it up on the Internet."

"Having more freedom sounds nice in theory, but I paid hundreds of thousands of dollars to become an [occupation] I'm not about to pour all that money down the drain."

"I'm already [insert total years in your current career] years in as an [occupation] and while I'd like to do something different it's too late for me to change my focus."

"If I was [age] instead of [insert your age] then maybe I'd make a change. It's just too risky right now."

"Honestly, I rather like being an [occupation]; it's not all bad. Yes, there are times that I daydream about doing "more" with my life but once I retire I can do those things. I just can't do them right now."

Chris & Tamsen: Please don't think that just because we wrote this book that we didn't have each one of these thoughts and probably at least thirty more we didn't list. We might as well be the poster children for jumping through the hoops of go to college, go to graduate school, get a good job, etc.

If you're having any of these thoughts don't worry each one of them is very normal at this point.

We want you to KNOW that "You've got this!" Keep reading and allow yourself to see each of these thoughts for the lies that they are. As you'll see in Chris' story you are so much more than your [occupation].

Real Life PB&J Story: Teacher

Chris: I'm a teacher, September through June. I teach and it's all I do. Period, the end...or so I thought. After fifteen years of firmly holding onto that belief, my wife unraveled it in thirty-seven minutes. Now I know that being a teacher *is part of who* I am, but it is not *all* that I am.

In Tamsen's constant quest to make others' lives better she had encouraged me many times to let her use her PB&J Course Design system to explore how I could take my teaching experience and create a PB&J product. And for every time she asked I responded with, "I'm not a course creator. That's what you do; it's not what I do. No thanks."

Fortunately (or unfortunately) for me she's relentless when she sees a glimmer of potential she refuses to quit. Honestly, she's truly gifted in her ability to take what's in someone's mind and transform it into an income stream.

Well, as I settled into my first morning of summer break blissfully enjoying the moment where I had nothing on my to-do list for the next three months ... Tamsen arrived with *my* to-do list in *her* hands.

As she laid out the list of where she needed my help, I felt completely overwhelmed. She desperately needed my help in her business. She was talking email lists, opt-ins, landing pages, courses, categories, posts ... I felt *totally* overwhelmed! I didn't want to enter her world. I didn't want to understand the language she was speaking. *I wanted to chill and enjoy my summer break!*

On Day 2 of "summer break", I headed to the gym at 3:30 a.m. (yes, that is my normal time!) On my way home, I was listening to Brendon Burchard's, The Charged Life, and as I listened to him talk about passion and how our passion can change the lives of others, my mind zoned out and I allowed myself to have a comfy chat with my thoughts.

"What was my passion?"

"What did I know that I felt could help others?"

Then "it" hit me like a ton of bricks - presenting!

I've been teaching kids how to put together class presentations for years. I have a system that works and one I am passionate about because I've seen first hand how this system helps parents and kids with classroom presentations.

I rushed into the house screaming - "Tamsen! Tamsen! I have an idea for my PB&J!" Within the hour, she was taking my idea through her (*brilliantly simply*) PB&J Course Design system, and in thirty-seven minutes, I *completely* smashed my former belief that my teaching was limited to September to June! She had taken my "presenting" skill and pulled out information I didn't even know I had in tucked away in my brain.

Honestly, the amount of information tucked away in those tiny little brain crevices was insane! Right before my eyes on the computer screen were multiple income streams for my one little idea. It was so easy to see how I could take my presenting skills and create a product to sell to twenty people* for $100 each month after month.

I'm eternally thankful for Tamsen's unwavering belief in the financial value of "me". That morning I moved from my limiting mindset of "Why me?" and "Why would anyone pay me for what I know?" to my new mindset (limitless by the way) of "Why not me?" and "Who wouldn't want what I have to offer?"

Chris Horton, Teacher | vacationinglife.com

*This was only one of my four income streams we created. My other levels of my digital product are FREE (to sample the product), $500, and $1,000.

HOW Work is Broken

Tamsen: Have you ever been on the receiving end of "it's me, not you" in a relationship about to take a turn you weren't expecting? Suddenly feeling overtaken by the suffocating feelings of disappointment, sadness, anger, devastation, and desperation to know what you could have done differently to "make things go back to the way they used to be".

Fortunately, there wasn't and isn't anything that you could've done differently because it truly was all about the other person. They wanted something that you couldn't give and by breaking up with you, they gave you the greatest gift they could—giving you the chance to go and find someone else who *could* give you everything you deserve and more.

Well, it's time for you to break up with HOW you work.

It's time for you to look "work" in the eyes and say, "It *is* you and I'm moving on" because you no longer live in a world where you are limited to trading your time for dollars.

Today, you have the opportunity to expand into different ways and types of work without ever having to leave what you're already doing behind.

When I broke up with "work" I felt (*and heard*) myself saying to "work", "It *is* you and I just *can't* do this anymore."

- I couldn't bear the thought of leaving my six-week old son to put on a suit and drive to a fancy downtown office to do the "lawyer gig" each day.

- I couldn't bear the thought of tracking my time in six-minute cycles so I could properly bill for the knowledge that I was pouring out of my brain for a client. (*Traditional law firm billing is done in six-minute increments.*)

- I couldn't bear the thought of having to see inefficiencies in the "system" and being unable to change them due to my place on the totem pole of authority.

You can enjoy what you do and still file for a *work divorce*.

Solutions typically show up in two ways -- in moments of inspiration or desperation.

I was desperate immediately following Kip's birth to find a way to use my extensive business experience and knowledge with my legal skills and somehow wrap the entire package in the fact that I was now a mother who wanted to raise her child.

I needed to find a *new* system that would allow me to share what I know and make money doing it with an infant on my lap. A system where I could trade the value of what I provided and not the time I spent "working."

So let me ask you before we get to the *new* system of "work":

- Would you be paid for your work if you didn't show up?
- If you stayed home, would you still get your paycheck?
- If you worked one hour or forty hours, would you make the same amount of money?

A New Way to Work

"When you grow up you tend to get told that the world is the way it is and your life is just to live your life inside the world. Try not to bash into the walls too much. Try to have a nice family life, have fun, save a little money. That's a very limited life. Life can be much broader once you discover one simple fact: Everything around you that you call life was made up by people that were no smarter than you. And you can change it, you can influence it... You can build your own things that other people can use. And the minute you can understand you can poke life .. you can change it, you can mold it. ... Once you learn that, you'll never be the same again." Steve Jobs, 1995

Tamsen: When I heard Steve Jobs say this he was speaking *directly* to me. In less than a minute he finalized the divorce between me and HOW I worked. Secretly, I wish I'd heard him in 1995 when he said this but my twenty-year-old self wasn't ready for such a *crazy* thought.

Fast forward to the summer of 2011 holding *baby* Kip in my arms, I was not only ready to hear it, I was ready to take action. Hmmm … no one any smarter than me had made everything around me?

What if I could make stuff? What if I could find a way to share what I know and make money doing it AND be a mother? The cascading sequence of "What if?" took over my entire afternoon and many afternoons since.

I did find a new way to "work" and in turn showed Chris and hundreds of other professionals how to do the same. This *new way* of working allows you to expand beyond any limitations of your current occupation and also tap into the unused resources of your talents and passions that can also become income streams (*if you want them to*) for your family.

It's time to expand your current life story.

It's time for you to learn how to make your digital product, your PB&J that you can share with the world and make money doing it.

What Can You Buy for $38?

Chris: How about a brand-new perspective on *what you can do* with fifteen years of career experience?

I want to shed some light on that little diabolical creature known as self-doubt, as I am enjoying my own PB&J adventure. At one time or another, we've all had self-doubt slip into our mind. I'm here to tell you for the low, low price of only $38, I cured myself of self-doubt. Thirty-eight dollars plus a little PB&J and I was on my way!

As part of her summer agenda, Tamsen asked me to help her figure out how to create an Amazon store for our Vacationing Life™ brand. I started investigating how to do that and quickly found self-doubt staring back at me from the computer screen. I seriously searched less than ten minutes and pretty much threw in the towel.

Not one to give up that easily, Tamsen suggested I look at an online course on 'How to setup your Amazon store.' I checked it out and after about thirty seconds clicked the Purchase Now button. Eagerly, I logged into the course and was excited to get rolling creating our Amazon store. The course opened and ... have you ever had that feeling like someone just piddled in your Cheerios?

I sat there, listening and watching, continuing to hope something good was going to come out of my $38. Patience ... wait ... give it another few minutes... Nothing! This course was a total bust for me. I was less than thrilled that I'd just sent this person $38 (*that's a BIG box of diapers!*) Then, it hit me. THIS WAS THE BEST $38 I HAVE EVER SPENT!

If this horribly recorded, *heavily* self-promoting live stream counted as a "course", I knew I COULD CREATE A COURSE MUCH BETTER THAN THIS! I was empowered, jazzed up, all kinds of awesome was pulsating through my veins because I'd seen what someone else was doing online and I knew I could totally make my own course better than what I had just spent $38 on.

Self-doubt defeated!

I am here to share with you, that if I (*Mr. Skeptical extraordinaire!*) can change my perspective about what is possible with my knowledge and skills, you can. If I can change my mindset about creating and taking my value out into the world, you can. You are only one PB&J away from a brand-new perspective.

Real Life PB&J Story: Faith & Business Coach

Before learning about Tamsen's PB&J Course Design system I had no experience, just a hope, and a dream. Being new to sharing what I love virtually was scary and was a huge leap. Tamsen was there every step of the way and made me excited to share what I believe is needed for the work at home woman of faith in today's media driven world.

The way Tamsen taught me how to organize my ideas with a mind map gave me the clear steps I needed to take to set up an online course that was easy for my customers to follow. I learned everything from how to create a recommended tools list to breaking the content down into bite-size steps that my customers could actively follow and gain results.

My first course, The Art of Purposeful Prayer Journaling, launched in July 2016 and I quickly enrolled my first ten customers. I chose to create this as my first PB&J product after a thoughtful process of elimination that I learned from PB&J Course Design. First, I brainstormed ideas that excited me into three different mind maps:

(1) a faith-based course,
(2) a homemaking course, and
(3) a sales course.

After really looking at what I myself needed before I felt ready to tackle another business venture, I realized that having a way to release insecurities and stress was in my own daily prayer journal. Creating The Art of Purposeful Prayer Journaling was exactly the product that I needed to make to help women continue on their path to giving themselves grace instead of trying to balance it all.

If there was ONE thing that I could leave you with it is that YOUR PB&J is important!

Once you learn how easy it is to make and then share it you'll be jumping at the opportunity to make it again and again. Tamsen clearly loves what she does to help others. Her mom-to-mom and wife-to-wife appeal is what originally sold me. It's genuinely who she is and her PB&J style. Her authenticity in wanting to help you harness and share your PB&J is real.

Genavieve Moyer, Faith & Biz Coach | bit.ly/ArtofPurposefulPrayer

Jelly Beans Before PB&J

"Life is short, and it is up to you to make it sweet."
Sarah Louise Delany

Tamsen: My legs are tingling and I'm doing very gentle ankle rolls to get some feeling back into my legs. I'm going into hour number four pinned into a recliner by my nine-pound baby boy. I don't dare move; quiet is far better than feeling my limbs, so I willingly stay captive. I've exhausted Netflix® and decide to take a trip over to YouTube®. Four minutes later, I'm silently weeping and wishing I could stay forever pinned by my nine-pound baby boy.

Four minutes ago, I stumbled across the viral sensation, Your Life in Jelly Beans, where 28,835 jelly beans spilled out on the floor *forever changed* how I saw my life.

Each jelly bean represented one day of life. As the video played, the creator removed small piles of jelly beans based on how many days of our lives we spend sleeping, working, watching TV, commuting, eating, taking care of friends and family, and a few other areas. Leaving viewers with the challenge - How will you spend what's left?

Weeping (*quietly of course due to sleeping baby*), I was thirty-six years old, a new mother, a lawyer, and a wife with NO idea what I was going to do with my life, my jelly beans. I felt ...

- sad because Kip was growing up so quickly,
- angry for wasting three years of college on a biology degree because I decided not to become a doctor,
- angry for wasting time on a career path that I never wanted,
- angry for finishing college a year early and missing out on so many memories,
- angry that I graduated law school at thirty-six and not twenty-six,
- frustrated that the legal profession was so backward,
- regret about becoming a lawyer,
- confused about what I could do,
- confused about what I should do,
- confused about what I wanted to do,
- overwhelming loss ... on all areas of my life

I felt like I was looking at a mountain of dirty laundry stacked thirty-six years high with no idea of where to even begin. Thirty-six years of decisions that had placed me where I was and I didn't like what I saw. Do I wash the clothes or toss them out and start all over? As the proactive type-A learner that I am, I started researching and working on a plan to tackle the massive pile of dirty laundry.

I found and fell in love with Danielle LaPorte's, *The Desire Map*. Inside its pages, I read about how to create a life not based on what I wanted to accomplish but instead on how I wanted to feel. Game changer! I soaked up every word and immediately started working on how I wanted to feel in my life. That massive pile of dirty laundry—well, it washed, folded, and put itself away in a little under twenty-four hours.

I could see my remaining jelly beans as the sweet treats that they were, and I set about deciding how I wanted to spend each and every one of them based on my feelings and not on the belief that work was hard, vacations were a few times a year and when I reached retirement age, life would be different. I'd believed all that for thirty-six years and I was moving on!

You have a decision to make right now because today is one of your jelly beans and tomorrow will be another, and another, and another.

Do you keep reading or close the book and continue to wonder "What if?"

- What if you could choose HOW you worked?
- What if you could choose work that fuels your soul?
- What if you could choose the people you spend the best hours of your day with?
- What if you could combine HOW you work with what you LOVE doing? (*two jelly beans for one in my opinion*)
- What if you could choose exactly how each of your remaining jelly beans is spent?

These are BIG questions and they are *worth* thinking about.

Snack Time: Count Your Jelly Beans

Take a handful of jelly beans and spread them out on a table. What do you see?

What I see is that there are many different colors and they easily move around on the table. We actually have a jelly bean dispenser in our home to remind us of how we're spending our time. When I need a *gentle reminder* I'll take a handful and spill the beans out onto the desk with Kip. We enjoy sorting the colors into piles and talking about what our favorite flavors are. *Kip really just enjoys eating them.*

In the *Your Life in Jelly Beans* video, the narrator offered the following percentages for how we spend the days of our lives. As you think about each area ask yourself these simple questions:

- How do you feel about that area right now?
- How do you want to feel about that area?
- Do you want MORE or less in that area?

29%	Sleeping
11%	Working
7%	Looking at a screen
6%	Eating and drinking
5%	Taking care of your home
4%	Commuting
2%	Community, civic, volunteer, or religious activities
2%	Personal grooming
2%	Taking care of friends and family
32%	Jelly beans remaining

When we looked at these percentages we wanted to not only *feel differently* about how we were spending our time but also *where we were spending* that time.

We started by intentionally choosing how our days were spent and the peanut butter we were creating. To estimate your own percentages, check out the exercise in the multimedia experience. (*If you live in Los Angeles you're commuting percentage is likely higher.*)

Your Peanut Butter

Carefully Choose Your Peanuts

"Knowing how you actually want to feel is the most potent form of clarity that you can have."
Danielle LaPorte

To make your PB&J product you need **your** peanut butter.

> **P = the peanut butter, which represents "Personality." All the pieces of you essential to creating the PB&J that's right for you. This is the gooey deliciousness inside you of who you want to be, how you want to live life, and how you want <u>to feel</u> each moment you are living life.**

Tamsen: Here's a challenge for you - please make one jar of peanut butter without using a single peanut. Kinda tricky, isn't it? Making peanut butter requires lots and lots of peanuts. Even if you're *allergic* to peanut butter and want a nut-free alternative, you're gonna need *a lot* of what you're using for the substitution.

Each day (*one jelly bean*) is the sum of all your feelings—
each one feeling similar to one little peanut that, when
blended together with others, create your life - your one
jar of peanut butter. The gooey deliciousness inside you
of who you want to be and how you want to live life.
You want to make sure you're choosing the right kind
of peanuts.

When we're talking about making your PB&J, your
peanut butter is made from your feelings instead of
peanuts -- even if you're allergic to peanuts, you're not
allergic to this book!

Now, you might be wondering, *why* use your feelings?
After all I don't remember *any* of my employers asking
me how I *felt* about the work I was being paid to do.
My feelings were simply not part of the work equation.
Feelings especially in terms of traditional "work," are
not an aspect that is often promoted or highlighted in
the workplace. They are actually most often frowned
upon and discounted in many ways.

That's one of the reasons that the current work system
is broken. Your feelings go with you every time you go
to work and they should factor into your life.

You use your feelings because your peanut butter is
made up of *how you want to feel each moment* you are living
life. P = the peanut butter and is your personality -- the

unique characteristics that make you who you are. When your personality is in alignment with how you want to feel each moment of your life then suddenly time flies by and you realize you've smiled all day. "Work" feels like playing, your soul is energized, and you're excited to do more!

We recently watched the Disney Pixar movie, *Inside Out*, with our son, Kip. As parents, we are eternally thankful to the creative geniuses who gave a physical form to joy, fear, anger, disgust, and sadness. We were able to help our son understand how feelings work. For the moment, Kip firmly believes that we all have joy, fear, anger, disgust, and sadness character figures running around and pushing buttons on a massive control panel right behind our eyeballs.

And you know what, he's right.

- How do you feel right now?
- How did you feel when you woke up this morning?
- How did you feel last week when the project you'd work so hard on received a round of applause from your boss and co-workers?
- How'd you feel watching your son or daughter hit their first home run?

Making Your Peanut Butter

*"If you don't plan on doing your job forever, than why
are you doing it now?"*
Simon Sinek

Tamsen: My Vitamix® blender arrived, and I couldn't
throw my almonds, walnuts, and pecans into the
blender fast enough. Finally, I could make my own
gourmet "peanut" butter. I was so tired of basic peanut
butter and wanted to create my own unique flavor by
choosing different nuts, adding a little vanilla, honey,
and chia seeds. The end result was delicious! I had
unleashed the potential to start making all kinds of
different "peanut butter."

Your peanut butter is determined by the feelings you
are choosing and tossing into the blender known as
your life. Just like I carefully chose the nuts I wanted to
use, you get to choose your feelings for today,
tomorrow, the next day, and the next.

- How carefully are you selecting your daily
  feelings?
- Are you intentionally choosing how you want
  to feel today?

Every day, we see brilliantly talented people *stuck*
believing that the only way to make peanut butter is to

use standard peanuts (*the default peanuts if you will*). No one has told them that they can choose different ingredients.

We've identified these as some of the default peanuts that we ourselves were using:

- "Fridays are fun and Mondays are miserable."
- "I wish I didn't have to go to work today."
- "We were lucky to find the jobs we had."
- "We'll pay our dues and then have fun when we retire."
- "We can't wait for our next vacation."
- "This is just the way it is."
- "We can't really change it so we'll make the best of it."

Snack Time: Choosing Your Feelings

Where are you taking default peanuts? Do you want to choose HOW you spend your days and how you FEEL during each day? You stop accepting the *default peanuts* by simply looking at *how* you want to feel throughout the day.

- How do you want to feel when you wake up each day?
- How do you want to feel going into work?
- How do you want to feel throughout your day?

- What are the feelings you want MORE of in your day?
- What are the feelings you want tossed to the side?

Tamsen: Let's face it, *we're all slightly nutty*. Each day, we add more feelings (*our peanuts*) to our lives. Every minute you live creates a feeling. What happens during those minutes creates your lifetime and that is why it is so very important to know how to use PB&J to help you *create more* of the feelings you want to have.

Now is the time to think about HOW do you want to *feel* when ...

- you're watching your kids smile and laugh,
- talking with a friend by the pool on a warm sunny day,
- planning a weekend getaway with your family, or perhaps the next family vacation,
- as you're getting ready to head out for work each day,
- coming home from work,
- you think about the people that really matter in your life,
- you're heading to the gym for your workout,
- you're at the best concert you've ever attended,
- your little ones head off to kindergarten, or graduate from high school, or leave for college,

- you hear for the first time you're going to be a parent, a grandparent, an aunt or an uncle,
- your boss tells you you're getting the promotion, recognition, or raise you've worked so diligently for,
- you see your baby take his first steps,
- you say "I do" to the love of your life,
- you pull out of your driveway in your car,
- you pull into the driveway of your home,
- you pack your suitcases to head out on your vacation.

Your Rearview Mirror

Tamsen: Let's imagine for a few moments that you're in your dream car, driving down the road on your way to your favorite vacation spot. As you're driving, so excited about what lies ahead, you also periodically check your rearview and side mirrors as you drive.

Those mirrors, and especially the rearview, help you safely arrive at your desired destination.

- Is it safe to change lanes?
- Is there anyone behind you that you need to watch out for?
- As you swerve to miss a tire in the middle of the road - you quickly glance in the mirror while exclaiming - "Whew! that was a close one!"

Just like in our real cars, we have a rearview mirror in our lives - the experiences, people, events, and awards - each serving an important role in helping you arrive here, right now, your destination for the moment.

I have no idea what you are feeling right now, but I know when I first thought about everything in my rearview mirror, it wasn't necessarily pretty. I felt mostly failure. Until I realized that I was really staring at my PB&J. My rearview mirror combined with PB&J is exactly what I needed to arrive at this moment with you.

So, let me ask you - What do you see in your rearview mirror? Let's take a little trip down Memory Lane and see what we can find. Whether you know exactly what lies behind you, or you have no idea what you've left behind, we're going to have a great trip.

As you start your trip, these are the areas that we're going to drive through: experiences, awards, skills, people, and proud moments. **When your memories come up know that whatever the memory is it's showing you the way to your PB&J.**

Experiences | "Are you sure?"

Have you ever had someone sprinkle a little doubt on your dreams?

Chris: "Are you sure you want to be a teacher?"

Nine little words may seem like a simple question that anyone might ask someone who is on the path towards becoming a teacher. In my case, this question rattled me.

I was in college and busy jumping through the educational hoops (i.e. classes) required to become a teacher, enjoying some classes while having the life dragged out of me by others. One class I really found joy in was an art class for elementary school teachers. I don't consider myself strongly skilled in the art department, but I do enjoy a good doodle, so I was pretty jazzed up about the class. Each class delivered more ideas of how I could use art in my own classroom one day.

One morning my professor gave me a new assignment - create a lesson for kids and find a classroom teacher willing to let me teach it. That sounded straightforward enough, and armed with my list of favorite lessons, I had a good idea of what I'd create. So, out I went on my journey to find a classroom teacher willing to lend me his or her class for forty-five minutes. Luckily, the first school I contacted had a principal who not only welcomed volunteers but also enjoyed a little bit of zest. Voila! Enter me, the zest!

It was spring of 1997 when I met the teacher whose students I would be borrowing and it was very clear that she was not a fan of the zest. She let me do my lesson anyway and I rocked it! I don't remember exactly what the lesson was, but I've never forgotten how I felt! I felt amazing! I knew I was in the right spot and that teaching was for me. I was excited and encouraged that I could use what I knew, connect with kids, and make a difference.

Immediately following my lesson, feeling alive and full of excitement, the non-zest-liking teacher approached me and asked, "Are you sure you want to be a teacher?" I was gut-punched right in the middle of my moment of JOY. I honestly didn't know how to react. The first thing that came to mind was, "Yes, of course."

You know there are all kinds people in your world. Some prefer zest; some are the anti-zest. Some are half-full, others half-empty. For some, today is a great day because of all the amazing zest in the world. That's where I choose to live, in the land of "today is amazing."

Her nine little words sprinkled a little self-doubt on my PB&J sandwich when I allowed her limitation to enter my mind.

That one question, those nine words, are now in my rearview mirror. I've grown as a person, and I've learned that another's perspective is a reflection of their experiences or limitations and not my own. Tamsen reminds me of this frequently.

Had I chosen to believe the self-doubt of that teacher, I wouldn't be a teacher. Instead of allowing the self-doubt to take hold and grow, I chose to redirect it and now challenge myself to be better year after year in the classroom.

That experience provided me the opportunity to see how another's perspective can impact how I see myself if I let it. This one experience gives me the fuel to help you make your own PB&J.

Limitations and doubts fade away; all you need is a little PB&J.

Snack Time: Experiences

Take some time and think about these questions because one of them might shine a light of clarity for you on what your PB&J is.

- What are the experiences in your rearview mirror?
- How did you feel in the middle of the experience?
- How do you feel now looking at it in your rearview mirror?
- What did you learn through your experiences that you could use in making your PB&J?

Awards | "Artic" Will Cost You a Happy Meal®

YOU are the only one that can make your PB&J, and *sometimes* it simply takes remembering the awards you've received to shine some well-deserved light on the PB&J you need to create.

Tamsen: In third grade, it was Zip's Ice Cream cones. In fourth grade, it was a McDonald's® Happy Meal®.

Those were the awards I craved as a child. In each of those magical school years, my motivation was to max out the award systems of my teachers. I still remember the first time Miss Jones took me to Zip's Ice Cream (*it was 1983 and going for ice cream with your teacher was totally okay*). I was so proud of myself for completing all the extra worksheets that she nicely laid out behind her desk.

Fourth grade became a bit trickier. My good friend Lisa, and I were in the same homeroom class. Our teacher, Mr. Smith, gave out a McDonald's Happy Meal as the reward for the student who earned a 100% on any test. Suddenly, I had competition with Lisa and I wanted that Happy Meal! I can still feel my gut sinking when I realized I left out the "c" in "arctic" and the "n" in "government"— and having to sit back and watch

Lisa eat her Happy Meal in class those days was the worst feeling in the world. But that experience also fueled a desire in me to do my best.

As adults, awards become trickier to collect.

Some awards are a true recognition of your skills and talent. Others simply require you to nominate yourself. And then there are the "awards" that are far more PR than an award. And when you receive the award - how much bragging is allowed?

Sure, winners of an Oscar® or a Super Bowl® can brag and shout their accomplishment from the rooftops; but what about regular people? Can we brag about our talents and skills?

Yes! Yes we can!

We'd like you to brag about yourself. You are incredibly valuable and the unique role you play in the world is exceptional.

An award I received as an adult caught me by surprise and is the one in my rearview mirror that provided just enough of a headlight beam to keep me safely on the road, but not too bright to freak me out. If I'd known what was coming ahead, I might have turned back. Much like becoming a mother—if I'd really known what being a mother meant—I probably would've said to Chris, "Let's buy fancy cars and take great vacations because I don't think I can be a mom," and I would've missed out on knowing two of the sweetest souls ever to live.

It was May 2010 and I was sitting next to Chris and his parents in the modern loft multi-purpose room of my law school for graduation awards night. Honestly, I went to the ceremony because I was so proud of myself for finally doing what I wanted to do with my education, and here it was - the finish line. I knew I was receiving awards for my grades (*whether as a little girl in third grade motivated by ice cream, or fourth grade by a Happy Meal – I've always strived to max out what I can do*), my role on a national Moot Court team, as well as being on the board of Law Review (*might sound fancy, but really was just a whole lot of extra work!*)

As the night went on, I gathered up many pieces of fancy paper (*knowing I'd quietly tuck them away for my sons to discover one day in a dusty box*). Leaving a career in trademark licensing three years earlier at age thirty-two didn't feel like such a scary idea any longer. I was so proud of myself. I'd graduated from law school. It was a very special night, to say the least.

Now you should know there is one award, given at the very end of the evening that is a secret. The winner is chosen by the faculty and staff and is typically the student body president, the highest grade point average, or someone that is highly active in many of the high visibility positions within the law school - NONE of which was me. Sitting in my chair, holding Chris's hand, listening as my good friend started sharing the story of the Leadership Award recipient ... it hit me ... she was talking about me! Holy crap. Holy Crap! Holy Crap! I'm a total sap and tears immediately started welling up in my eyes, much like they are doing right now as I am sharing this story with you.

I remember shaking as I walked to the front of the very large room with a couple hundred pairs of eyes on me...me! As the beautiful crystal award was placed in my hands, I felt nothing and everything all at once. I'd never considered myself a leader and it took me a couple of years (*remember headlights just bright enough to keep me headed in the right direction but not so bright that I freaked out?*) to realize that I am a leader and always have been.

Today, I'm very proud to say that I'm living up to what the award represents—embracing how to find solutions that don't yet exist, willing to ask "what if?" and "why not?" and then carefully making the very best map I can to help others navigate their own path.

Snack Time: Awards

Between you and yourself write down your answers to these questions because one might hold the answer for you about the PB&J that is inside of you waiting to come out.

- What awards have you earned?
- How did you feel when you earned them?
- How do you feel now when you think about them?
- What were the awards for?
- What did the award stand for?
- In looking at the award, *HOW* can it help you make your PB&J?

Skills | Where do you ROCK?

What can you do better than anyone else?

Have you perfected the coconut macaroon? Or do you know the best way to teach a child to tie their shoes?

Tamsen: When I started really breaking down my PB&J Course Design system it was shocking to me how many people were shelling out thousands of dollars to learn from other people and yet saw zero financial value in their own skill set. Now I know it's because when something is easy for us (*even if we took a long time to learn it*) we take it for granted and the self-doubt creeps in wondering "Who would pay for this?"

Lots of people will pay you for the PB&J you make but first, you need to take inventory on your unique skill set and part of that is sharing with you that your PB&J might just be fried chicken as it was for Colonel Harland Sanders the creator of Kentucky Fried Chicken®.

The day after reaching retirement, Harland feeling entirely overwhelmed by the failure of his life, he sat down to write his Last Will & Testament. Instead, he started a list of the things he hadn't yet done. Sitting under a tree in the heat of summer he realized he knew how to make great fried chicken! So he got up and went and made his secret recipe fried chicken and sold it to his neighbors. Well, you know the rest of the story -- Kentucky Fried Chicken is now a multi-billion dollar business and all because instead of cashing in his chips, Colonel Sanders made a list of his skills. You can watch the full story unfold; go to www.colonelsanders.com

Even Kip, our five-year-old, has unique skills he's developed and could share with other kids - his PB&J. He has a natural talent and deep enjoyment for crafts. Every day he makes amazing inventions and beautiful art with egg cartons, yarn, and any other item that others may consider "trash." He could seriously run

Kip's Crafting Class and we're pretty sure he'll have his own section in our Vacationing Life store before kindergarten is finished.

Snack Time: Where do you ROCK?

What talents or interests do you have in your skill set? The skills set questions are particularly helpful for anyone in a skilled trade: electrician, plumber, ceramic tile installation, hardwood flooring installation, hair stylist, makeup artist, etc.

- What do you know how to do that you could teach someone else?
- How did you feel learning that skill?
- How do you feel now, knowing you have this skill as part of your talents?
- How does this skill impact your everyday life?
- How could this skill impact your everyday life?

Who knows? Maybe you have the recipe for the best peanut butter and jelly sandwich the world has ever tasted!

People | Who is your "Aunt Pat"?

Tamsen: In the summer of 2004, life reconnected me with my Aunt Pat and Uncle Mike whom I adored since childhood. As I was growing up, every single visit with them was etched into my rearview mirror as happy, fun, and all laughter:

- While I was in second grade they came to Ft. Worth, Texas and watched me roller skate on the driveway. My aunt was the most beautiful woman I'd ever seen. She had a denim dress, boots, and a *super-cool* cowboy hat.

- During my fourth grade year, they came to my biological father's graduation from medical school and took me to a fancy Italian restaurant where I had linguini and a kiddie-cocktail for the first time.

- For my thirteenth birthday, I spent a week with them in New York City going to museums, having champagne at the Russian Tea Room, seeing the Nutcracker, skating at Rockefeller Center, and a very special trip to Tiffany's.

- When I was eighteen, it was a wonderful week at the family shore house swimming at Ocean Beach Club and playing tennis with my four-year-old cousin, Bo.

Due to various family events far outside my control, I hadn't been in touch with them for about six years, but they'd always had an incredibly special place in my heart.

I still remember that moment in 2004 as if it was yesterday, seeing my Aunt Pat, hugging her, and somehow *deeply knowing* that everything was going to be all right; *I was finally home.* **That moment, that hug, that afternoon twelve years ago was my one-person moment that changed everything for me.**

We quickly found ourselves on the patio at their hotel, in Muskegon, Michigan, of all places and as life often has a funny way of doing, years of stories came tumbling out of me. There's really nothing like doing a semi-complete rundown of your rearview mirror experiences in a matter of a few hours. I was working in collegiate trademark licensing and I remember my aunt asking, "So, what is next?" as only she could do. "Where is this going?" Honestly, I had no idea.

By November of that year, I was flying to their home to spend Thanksgiving with them.

By the end of the long holiday weekend, plans were in motion for me to start heading to law school. I'll never forget the conversations my aunt and I had while happily shopping in downtown Princeton where I shared with her that I'd *thought about* going to law school. She didn't skip a beat; she never does.

"Alright," she said, "you're thirty years old now, and I don't think you want to start much past thirty-two, so what do we need to do?"

Now you need to know that **my aunt is brilliant, elegant, and the finest example of a wife, mother, and woman that you'll ever meet**. She was an investment banker before Bo, her son, was born, and, while in college, received a full scholarship to Yale Law School that she declined because she wanted to be on the deal-making side of business.

Never in my life had *anyone* taken what I wanted to do seriously. I wasn't even taking it seriously because, after all, I was thirty. *People don't go to law school at thirty.* They stay in their jobs, pay their bills, hope to get married, have a couple of kids, and do life. Looking back in my rearview mirror, I see how misguided that belief system was, but it's what I used to navigate my life. *Little did I know that I was about to dive headfirst into living a PB&J life.*

Well, as you already know, I am a lawyer and the fact that you are reading this book is because of Aunt Pat. Without her and her love, financial resources, and unconditional support for me over the past twelve years, this moment right here with you wouldn't exist.

Snack Time: Who is your "Aunt Pat"?

Life has a beautiful way of bringing people into our lives that come alongside and make an impact on not only WHO we are but also WHERE we are.

- Is there someone in your life that came alongside and made an impact on you, resulting in where you are right now?
- Did they see something in you that you couldn't see?
- What did they see in you that you couldn't see?
- How did they help get you to where you are today?
- Where do you think you'd be without them?
- What role did they play in your PB&J?

If you have an Aunt Pat in your life, when was the last time you told them thank you? I bet they'd really like to hear it.

- Send a text.
- Take a picture and send it.
- Write a note and mail it.
- Make a phone call.
- Send an email.
- Order a gift basket.
- Stop by for a visit. *I'm incredibly jealous on this one. I'd give anything to stop by for a visit. When you do,*

take a picture and tag me on Instagram @vacationinglife #auntpat – I'd love to meet your "Aunt Pat". After all it's the "Aunt Pats" that change the world!

Proud | Dive Rings Beat Video Games

Chris: Summer nights for our family are spent at the pool. Kip and I swim and jump off the diving board for hours each night. The deep end of the pool is twelve feet, and that's a long way to swim for a five-year-old boy. Each night, we work our way deeper and deeper into the pool by diving for toys.

We talk underwater to each other, make silly faces, and even dance—seriously simple fun times with my little boy. One evening as we were playing, I threw some dive rings over the rope into the deep end. As we started to go after them, I realized one went a bit too far and landed in the deepest part of the pool. I planned on going down to get it, but before I knew it, Kip was heading down!

I quickly got my head underwater so I could see his little body gracefully moving in the water towards the ring that landed deep, deep down to the bottom. His hand reached out and he snagged it from the bottom of the pool! Then, his feet hit the bottom of the pool and he rocket-launched himself up to the surface! Holy cow! I was right there waiting for him when he surfaced and looked at him, swelling with pride and excitement, playing it cool. I simply said, "Did you get it?" He showed me the ring and smiled. I told him how awesome that must have felt and we continued to play.

On our way home from the pool, Kip says, "You know what guys?" *(that's what he typically says from his seat in the "trunk" (3rd row) of the mini-van to Tamsen and I in the front seats)*.

"You know that time we went to that place to play all of those games?" (referring to Dave and Buster's restaurant). When I went to the bottom of the pool, it felt better than playing all of those games."

Wow! Tamsen and I shot glances of surprise at each other. A honest-to-goodness example him feeling proud of himself. A deep-down feeling that only Kip could truly appreciate. He felt an internal pride that was amazing and we could hear it in his voice and it was clearly written all over his face.

The coolest part of Kip's experience of grabbing the dive ring from the bottom of the deep end was that now he has a point of reference for when we talk about what it means to be proud of yourself. Now when Tamsen creates a book, a guide, or a course that she's worked very hard on, Kip understands what she means when she says she's proud of herself.

If I come home from teaching and am excited to share a story about one of my underdog students doing something amazing, now Kip can relate and understand that daddy is proud of himself. Kip can now tie emotions to words based on his experience.

Snack Time: Time to Dive!

Do you have a "dive ring" moment in your life? A moment where you *felt* overjoyed by an accomplishment.

- What are you most proud* of?
- How did you feel in the moment?
- How do you feel now thinking about that moment?
- What events led up to what you are most proud of?
- How can what you are proud of find its way into your PB&J?

*Other words to help you identify the proud moments in your life: pleased, happy, glad, delighted, satisfied, or overjoyed.

Real Life PB&J Story: Video Consultant

Before using PB&J Course Design, making a digital product to sell took a *really* long time. Each time I wanted to create a product to share with my customers the entire experience was a massive experiment in patience that I felt I had to trudge through because I didn't have a systematic way to efficiently organize my content and then turn it into a paid product.

After using the PB&J system, all I can say is IT WORKS and I will *never* create another course alone again! PB&J Course Design saves my time and sanity by giving me a step-by-step reusable system to create powerful, impactful online courses (or presentations, or books, or videos) that help educate and change the lives of my clients.

I've now used PB&J Course Design twice with Tamsen. We worked together to create two online courses both having multiple price points. After seeing hundreds of my VIP members embarrassed by the "look" of their YouTube® channel, something Tamsen herself struggled with, we created an online training course to help business owners create a YouTube® channel that they wanted to scream about (in the very best way!)

After the ease and success of my first PB&J experience, Tamsen and I worked together to revamp a training that I had offered both as a free and paid product. She helped me create four different price points for my Video P.A.S.S. (*plan a system and a strategy*). Knowing how important it is for me to help my customers create a Business Cinema™ experience for my customers, and not have them making videos all willy nilly – we truly collaborated on the solutions that would equip my customers with exactly what they need short- and long-term in their video journeys.

When you have expertise in an area, it's often difficult to recognize what others don't know or what they might be struggling with. Having another person, specifically one as smart as Tamsen, to bounce my ideas off of and ask questions was worth its weight in gold! Collaborating with her helped me see how easily I could share my expertise, as easy as making a peanut butter and jelly sandwich.

Holly Gillen, Your Go-To Video Gal |
www.hollygstudios.com

Ideal Day

Tamsen: It was 6:04 a.m. Kip and I were awake, and I glanced at my phone sitting on the kitchen counter. There was a missed call and a voicemail from Aunt Pat at 5:04 a.m. I consider my aunt and uncle my surrogate parents, and it was really unusual for them to call that early. I played the voicemail and it simply said, "Sweetheart, it's Aunt Pat. Call me." Both Chris and I thought that her father, whom we adored, had passed away. I called her back and what I heard was the last thing I ever expected.

Bo is dead.

Bo is my cousin who I loved as a brother. A brother that I never fought with always adored and loved unconditionally. The one who sat perched on a snowy cliff while we were on vacation in Vail, Colorado laughing hysterically as I was upside down in a snow bank—forget coming to my rescue. He was only twenty-four years old. I froze and handed the phone to Chris. My world changed instantaneously. Looking down at Kip, who was two years old at the time, holding onto the leg of my pajama pants, I felt nothing and everything at that moment.

There will be more stories about Bo and the life that he lived in his short twenty-four years. He was a silent, selfless, national hero who squeezed every single ounce out of life. In the days that passed, my soul gave birth to what Chris and I know as Vacationing Life. We weren't going to waste or miss another single day. We would create a life for ourselves and the boys that honored Bo's memory and live each day to the fullest.

In the years that followed, we've done just that. We've created a life that feels like a vacation. No one knew how to "do vacations" better than Bo. He was a loving, real-life example of living guided by his soul and what he loved. He gave everything, including his life, so that we could be sitting at our family desk in the front room of our lovely home making PB&J products and living our Vacationing Life.

We hope that you've not had to experience a moment like we did on March 2, 2014, but reading this book is a moment for you.

You have today. You have this time to intentionally create your ideal days and start living them now.

What's the one-day you consider your BEST DAY EVER?

One day when life exceeded all your expectations. A day when time moved slowly, in the best possible way because you didn't want it to end? A day that you play over and over in your mind, cherishing each moment because of how amazing you felt.

When was the last time you relived that day, looking through pictures, playing the movie of memories in your mind, or reminiscing with someone who was there with you?

You see, making PB&J gives you the freedom to live your ideal day over, and over, and over. Never again are you restricted to looking through photos or replaying the day in your mind. You can totally do all of those, and we hope you do, but we want to help you create a life of ideal days strung together.

Now is the time to open your mind and allow yourself to dream really big. If you're anything like Chris and me, it's pretty easy to determine surface level goals: how many vacations a year, how much in the emergency fund, how much in the retirement accounts, new furniture to buy, house renovations we'd like, etc.

But after March 2, 2014, we knew our dreams were too small. We weren't living our ideal day and that was going to change permanently.

You deserve to spend each of your jelly bean days exactly the way you want. Make each day so full of experiences, events, people, and conversations that you fill up your social media feeds with nothing but joy. As Abraham Lincoln said, the best way to predict your future is to create it. Right now in your hands is the tool, the cheerleading squad, and the excitement to start creating your ideal days.

As parents, we'd love to say sit down and set aside time to really think about what you want; but let's get real—that doesn't happen! We're guessing your life is as busy as ours, so we're offering our methods of how to actually make the design of your ideal day happen and we'll pop them in where they make sense. The ideal day exercise allows you to step back and realize, "Oh my goodness, like, I can make my ideal day a reality? I really can do this?" Yes, you can!

What you're doing is designing your life into existence, really thinking about, "What does my ideal day look like?"

Snack Time: Ideal Day

Start with a day, a memory, or even a vacation that was your BEST DAY and write out the details.

- Where were you?
- Who were you with?
- What were you doing?
- What did you eat?
- Did you have amazing drinks?
- What was the best part of the day?

Our best day ever was before the boys were born; we weren't even married yet. My aunt and uncle took Bo, my brother Chip, Chris, and me to Virgin Gorda in the British Virgin Islands. After visiting the islands for over twenty years, my aunt decided that it was time to rent a villa and boy, did she choose a winner. Our home for one week was the Villa Aquamare, right on the beach of Mahoe Bay. We spent our days together, laughing, swimming and playing Uno® in the infinity pool, kayaking (*and tipping over ... yes, there is some good snorkel gear at the bottom of Mahoe Bay, courtesy of Chris!*) and having the best dinners prepared by Mimi, our chef.

One night as we all were sitting around the dinner table, my Uncle Mike said, "Okay, well out of that whole trip, what was the best day?" Everyone's answer was the day when we went island hopping on the Pampered Pirate with Elton and Pops. My aunt, uncle, and Bo have known Elton for twenty years and it was incredible to finally meet the gentle soul that I'd grown up hearing about. There was snorkeling in caves, Chris pulling the boat to shore on Jost Van Dyke, and freaking Elton out when he picked up the anchor! (Chris is a former power-lifter and loved every second of the "Holy cow! You can do that?!" moment.)

This was and still is one of our best days.
- How do we live like this in our real life?
- How do we take that ideal day and make it our everyday?

You take a step back, analyze, and practically recreate the elements you want to experience each day by writing down the experience of the "ideal day" and then finding a way to recreate those feelings in your "every day".

Ideal day: we woke up together in a beautiful room listening to the crashing waves of Mahoe Bay and all cuddled up in amazing sheets.

> Every day: we have a sound machine with ocean waves and our favorite bamboo sheets from our favorite hotel. Right now we're not waking up together, but instead next to one of our boys; for right now, that's heaven.

Ideal day: we had delicious breakfasts and could sit on the porch watching the water all while quietly waking up with perfectly selected music by Uncle Mike.

Every day: we turn on Jack Johnson on an iPad® with Spotify® radio, quietly letting everyone wake up, and cooking either oatmeal with fresh fruit, eggs, or making green smoothies.

Ideal day: we spent the day on the Pampered Pirate, drinking Heineken, and having rum and cokes with crackers and cheese; laughing, oh so much laughing; jumping off Willy T's into the crystal blue water while having lunch (Chris, Bo, and my brother jumped - I did not!)

Every day: our local party store now stocks Pusser's Rum for us, so we can have rum and cokes; we tried to buy Heineken but it's not the same in the U.S. as it is in the islands; we often make appetizer dinners and sit on our screened in porch; and as often as we can, we go to the beach!

Ideal day: we had a beautiful outdoor shower with plumeria flowers covering the ceiling and the smoothest pebbled flooring beneath our feet, the shampoo was divine!

Every day: (no outdoor shower as we live in Michigan) so the sand, seashells, and framed ocean pictures bring Mahoe Bay home, and

Chris found out the exact brand and scent of the toiletries while we were there—Bvlgari Green Tea—and orders shampoo, conditioner, body wash, etc. for me. I keep one bar of the soap on our desk and anytime I need to escape, the islands are one deep breath away.

So, that's what ideal day vs. every day looks like. What about Mondays, Wednesdays, and regular weekends? Yes, we're going to create those!

What does your ideal Monday look like? As one-half of a family that has designed our ideal day, I can say that I often forget that Monday is Monday until I start seeing social media posts on Sunday evenings about friends wishing the weekend wasn't over. I want to encourage you—if you want to live your ideal Monday, you can. You can live an ideal week!

To get started, answer the following questions. I recommend starting with Monday, Wednesday, and Saturday.

- What time are you waking up?
- Is an alarm clock waking you up, or do you wake up on your own?
- Where are you waking up?
- Who are you waking up next to?
- What does your bedroom look like?

- What sounds and smells are around you?
- What do you do when you wake up?
- What are you having for breakfast?
- Do you go to the gym, do yoga, or just chill?
- What time do you leave for work?
- Where are you working?
- What does your commute look like?
- What are you doing as you make your way into work?
- Who are you working with?
- What are you most looking forward to doing?
- What does your working space look like?
- How do you feel in your working space?
- How long are you working before lunch?
- Where are you having lunch?
- What are you having for lunch?
- Who are you having lunch with?
- How long are you enjoying your lunch?
- What do you do after lunch?
- How do you feel as you go through your afternoon?
- What is your commute home like?
- Do you stop somewhere on your way home?
- When you arrive home, how do you feel?
- What are you doing when you arrive home?
- Who is waiting for you when you get home?
- What do you have for dinner?
- Where are you having dinner?
- Who are you having dinner with?

- What happens after dinner?
- What do you love most about your evenings?
- What time are you going to bed?
- Who are you going to bed with?
- How do you feel in your bedroom at night?
- What are the sounds and smells surrounding you?
- What do you do as you are going to sleep?
- Do you dream?
- What do you dream about?

With the ideal day exercise now a part of your life experience, anytime you are enjoying an experience, you can think about practical ways to bring that time home with you and make the ideal day your everyday.

- Love the sheets at the hotel you're staying at? Ask the hotel if you can purchase a set.
- Love the toiletries? Find out the brand, and see if you can order them online.
- Have an amazing drink? Ask the bartender what he or she used, and buy what you need.
- Love the views? Go shopping and see if you can buy a picture to bring home with you.

I wake up every day looking at a Christmas ornament that I bought in Virgin Gorda, spray a little Bvlgari Green Tea perfume, wake up on bamboo sheets, and remember that I need to reorder the shampoo from

Disney's Contemporary Resort—this is how you make ideal days into every day.

Take a picture of a piece of your ideal day and tag us on Instagram @vacationinglife #idealday

Real Life PB&J Story: Attorney

Easy As PB&J is helping me keep my online course simple and easy to consume. As an attorney, it is easy for me to quickly wander off into legal jargon. Using what Tamsen and Chris have laid out is helping me easily organize my thoughts and ideas in a way that I know everyone will be able to follow and enjoy.

Before Tamsen shared *Easy As PB&J* with me I struggled to create content that I could share with others and make money doing it. I didn't have a starting point. I didn't even know how to brainstorm the idea. It was if the idea would hang out in my thoughts and then I would give up because it was too hard.

Now I know that anyone can create a PB&J! I'm currently researching law to help me create an online training course for entrepreneurs focused on the wedding industry. Helping them understand how to create a business structure, which contracts they need to keep their business safe, and other laws that they wouldn't know about because it's not their area of expertise but it is mine!

I'm not only using *Easy As PB&J* to create an online course but also a presentation and a book. I'm going to use this system for everything because as an attorney, time equals money and spending an hour developing an idea is a great use of my time!

Anyone can do this! You don't have to be an attorney or a professional at what you want to do. You just have to have an idea and passion … and a little PB&J helps a lot!

Samantha Meza, Attorney | www.sjflaw.net

Be.Do.Have.

Tamsen: "Stick to math and science. Writing just isn't your thing."

I still remember hearing those words thousands of times as a child. Every time I had to diagram a sentence, write a short story, or analyze a literary work, I hated it. *Life sure has a sense of humor.*

In the early hours of my day, when the boys are asleep and Chris is at the gym, I write in my journal. I write down all kinds of thoughts; some random and some organized. Sometimes the writings are life-related, sometimes business-related.

One morning my shaking hand wrote, "I am a New York Times Best-Selling Author."

Holy crap! I didn't just write that down! No, I didn't. Ugh, it's in ink now—momentary freak-out happening—and at the same time, *I knew I had to* write, "I am a New York Times Best Selling Author" in my journal that morning.

The thought had floated in my mind long enough and finally that little girl inside me who had been told over and over that writing wasn't her thing had the courage to write down "I am a New York Times Best Selling Author" on a single journal line that *no one would ever see.*

I'd listened to the Be.Do.Have exercise playing over and over again in my ears for the past eighteen months. As part of a product I purchased from Denise Duffield-Thomas, author of Lucky Bitch, she had included the ever-popular self-discovery Be.Do.Have exercise. I'd written down all kinds of "I want to be a [blank]" statements, but *never quite had the courage* to write down the one "be" continually wiggling around in my mind. I knew what I really wanted to be. I was simply too afraid to put pen to paper and write what only my children might stumble upon in a dusty journal after my death.

Be.Do.Have three little words, much like PB&J, holding all kinds of power to unlock doors of possibilities and potential in your life.

As you start going through this material, we'd encourage you to do this work with your #hometeam family. It's always interesting to see what's just beneath the surface of our loved ones and friends when we simply give each other the permission and time to share their thoughts.

#hometeam = the friends and family you consider your "family." You'll hear us talking about your home team throughout the book because Easy As PB&J is a team affair.

We are having such fun teaching the boys these concepts and showing them they can Be.Do.Have whatever they want, and teaching them *they need to own* what their desires are and not sacrifice for anyone. We are building the vocabulary of Be.Do.Have into the language they speak and understand.

Be.

Tamsen: You've already discovered one of my "Be" items—being a New York Times Best Selling Author—and how scared I was to write it down in my journal. I didn't start with that sentence. I started by listing all the things I already was because that was much easier and somehow gave me permission and security to start writing out what I really wanted to be.

My starting list:
- I am a wife.
- I am a mother.
- I am a lawyer.
- I am a business owner.

- I was a figure skater.
- I was a figure skating coach.
- I was a law professor.
- I played the violin, flute, and piano.

Snack Time: Who do you want to be?

As you start writing your list, start with who you are today.

- Are you a parent?
- Are you a niece or nephew?
- What do you do for work?
- Did you, or do you play a sport?
- Did you, or do you play an instrument?
- Are you married?

Your list is unique and important. Now you can use that list and add to it:

- Who do you want to be?
- What do you want to be?

As you're writing out your answers, you might run into thoughts like I did:

- "I can't be that."
- "Well, I'd like to be that, but I'll settle for this instead."
- "That's so arrogant. I can't write that down."
- "That will never happen."

- "How could I even think I could be that?"

Let me encourage you to respect what you're feeling, but know that none of it is true. I've learned this myself over and over in the last forty-one years—what I was taught about who I could be and what I could be was largely based on the limitations and beliefs of plenty of well-meaning people in my life.

Even now there are many people in my life, *fewer each year* that would scoff at me saying, "I am a New York Times Best-Selling Author." But it doesn't matter what they think. What matters is how I see myself and how I can take a sliver of courage and write out what I'd like to be in the quiet security of my journal.

So write ...write in the quiet security of where you put your thoughts and ideas. Let your own version of "I am a New York Times Best Selling Author" scare you for now, but don't let it stop you from writing it down. After all, no one is ever going to read it...or will they?

<u>Do.</u>

Tamsen: Once you're pumped and excited, and maybe even a little scared about what you want to be, now you're going to make a list - What do you want to do?

Much like I divided the "be" into what I already am and what I'd like to be, I like to do the same with "DO." So often, we take for granted things we've done. **We forget to assign the value of what we've done.** In high school, I chose Japanese as my foreign language because the boy I liked was in the class. I ended up really enjoying the language and over the summer between my junior and senior years of high school earned a scholarship to travel to Japan.

Now when I look at my list of what I want to do, traveling to different places shows up frequently. Chris and I want to take the boys to locations of the events they'll study in school, to show them firsthand artwork, battle sites, and architecture that makes up their world. Going to Japan and living there impacted what I wanted to DO with my life and my boys.

Snack Time: What do you want to do?

Your turn—listing what we've already done is so powerful:

- Where have you traveled?
- What have you seen?
- What have you done in your life?
- How did you feel doing these things?

While reading the obituary of a childhood friend who died five years ago, it quickly reminded me that we have to get busy doing. He was only thirty-seven years old. My cousin Bo was twenty-four. Please get busy doing exactly what it is you want to DO.

- What do you want to do?
- Do you want to travel?
- Do you want to learn a foreign language?
- Maybe learn how to cook?

"Doing" Without Leaving Your Living Room

"What you focus on expands. So focus on what you want, not what you do not want."
Esther Jno-Charles

Kip: "Mommy, can I watch the Evans family?"
Me: "Sure Kip. Where are they going today?"
Kip: "Mickey's boat."

As we write out our #hometeam list of what we want to do we typically look on YouTube® and find a video we can watch. Then we add those videos to a playlist and any time we want to quickly live the experience all we have to do is click play.

This simple act of watching videos has strengthened our family bonds because we can watch the videos together. When Kip told us that he wanted to go on Mickey's boat (Disney Cruise) for Christmas we didn't hesitate to pull up a video and see exactly what that would look like.

Maybe you have ten minutes while you're waiting in line. Think about one thing you'd rather be doing right then, get on your phone, open up the YouTube® app, find a video, and watch it. Immediately transport yourself to what you'd rather be doing—trust me, it's powerful!

Have.

Tamsen: Here, I think this is the spot. Yes, this is it! Trip number (*at least*) fifty-eight, and I think this is it.

It's 8:35 a.m. on a *regular* Thursday morning and I'm standing on an empty piece of land feeling the grass beneath my feet, the morning sun dancing on the glass reflection of the lake, and watching twenty little sailboats out for the morning sailing lesson. The cool breeze smells like fresh water, and no one else is awake...except for us.

Kip, "Mom, what are you doing?"
Me: "Deciding where to put the beach house, honey."
Kip: "Ok."

Our beach house. The one where I'll have my morning coffee waiting for the boys to tumble out of bed and join me downstairs on the screened-in porch where Chris and I are sitting working on the latest PB&J project for Vacationing Life. The one where my grandchildren will hold my hand as we walk down to Lake Michigan to play in the sand. Yes, this is it.

You see, every single one of us—Chris, Kip, Tad, and me—are happiest when there is sand between our toes and wind blowing through our hair. I first noticed it in Kip when he was not quite two years old. I'd taken him to the beach to play and he ran for hours and often started simply rolling around in the sand. His spirit was different.

Having a beach house *is essential* for my family.

What would you really, really like to have? So often we think, I have this [thing], *but* I'd really like to have this one.

- I have this car, *but* what I really want is ...
- We live here, *but* where we'd really like to live is ...
- I work here, *but* where I'd really like to work is...

Years ago, I heard Oprah say that when you use the word "*but*", erase everything that came before it because you just made it irrelevant. Now, that little list above quickly becomes:

- ~~I have this car, but~~ **What I really want is ...**
- ~~We live here, but~~ **Where we'd really like to live is ...**
- ~~I work here, but~~ **Where I'd really like to work is ...**

Now, looking at the sentences ~~with the strikethrough~~, it's easy to identify what you want to have.

Snack Time: What do you want to have?

What would you like to "Have" in your life?

Start by writing down all that you already have in your life. As you write it down, say "thank you." Expressing gratitude in your life, according to Robert A. Emmons, Ph.D., a leading gratitude researcher, is key to a fulfilling and healthy life. Do you have a:

- Job?
- Car?
- Home?
- Bike?
- Furniture?
- Jewelry?
- Computer?
- Other?

Honor what you have. Write it down and then say thank you for it.

For example, I'd write in my journal -- "We have a beautiful home. Thank you for a home that is warm when it's cold outside and cool when it's hot outside. Thank you for plenty of space for the boys to play. Thank you for the safety of the cul-de-sac, the miles of bike trail to ride our bikes, easy access to grocery stores, hospitals, schools, and grandparents."

By writing down what you currently "have" and expressing thankfulness for it, you are laying the foundation to expand and grow from there.

What comes after the "but"? As you look at your list, is there a "but" that you'd add to the sentence?

For us, "we have a beautiful home *but* we'd like a different floor plan." We're saying "Yes, we love where we are. We enjoy where we are, *but* we'd like to have an indoor basketball gym." We live in Michigan and winters are long. We have two active boys and we'd like to encourage activity long-term. As open house junkies, we've now seen two lovely homes both with indoor basketball courts and that feature is now non-negotiable on our "have" list.

Is having an indoor basketball gym ridiculous and totally unnecessary? It might be for other people, but it's not for us.

"*But* we can't 'have' that!"

As you're writing down the cars, homes, jewelry, computers, vacations, etc. that you'd like to have, you may run into limiting beliefs. **A limiting belief is a thought you have that stops you from acting, doing, or choosing something you'd otherwise select.**

The concept of limiting beliefs was not something that neither Chris nor I grew up knowing about but when we read *Think and Grow Rich* by Napoleon Hill we learned how restricted our lives were based on our limiting beliefs. *If you haven't read Think and Grow Rich, we highly recommend it.*

Snack Time: Crush the Limiting Beliefs

It's often difficult to identify your limiting beliefs. We use this exercise in conjunction with Be.Do.Have because it helps target the limiting beliefs.

- On a sheet of paper, put what you want to have in the center of the paper*.

- On the left-hand side of the paper, list all the reasons you'd like to "have" what you wrote down. Also, add in how you'd feel if you had the "thing" that you wrote down.
- On the right-hand side of the paper, list all the reasons and thoughts you have about why you can't "have" what you wrote down.

You can see a visual example of this Snack Time in the multimedia experience.

The right-hand side of the paper is the limiting beliefs you have about what you want to "have."

We definitely had to *fight through* our own set of limiting beliefs when it came to wanting to "have" a beach house *and* a home in the city with an indoor basketball court. *If you'd like to see our limiting belief work on this "have" you can see it within the multimedia experience.*

Here were some of the limiting beliefs that we ran into:

- "We don't really need a beach house."
- "Only crazy rich people have a beach house and a regular house."
- "What will our friends think if we have a house on Lake Michigan?"
- "I can't want a beach house."
- "I can't have a beach house."
- "Some of our friends won't like us if we do this."

You will have your own limiting beliefs and it's important to understand that these thoughts are false. As Louise Hay, of

Hay House Publishing, says, "We learn our belief systems as very little children, and then we move through life creating experiences to match our beliefs." *Thousands* of people have a beach house, why not us?

The other day, we were leaving the pool and there was an Audi R8 parked at the edge of the parking lot. Chris noticed it and said, "Oh my gosh, that's an Audi R8!" "Oh", was my unimpressed response ... I had to Google it. As you can probably guess, that car is not on my HAVE list. The driver of that car probably had it on his or her HAVE list.

That's the beauty of Be.Do.Have; you write down what you want to have. Doesn't matter what anyone else thinks... no one will ever see your list ... be warned, the Universe does have a sense of humor as evidenced by the fact that you are right now reading some thoughts I never thought would escape the privacy of my journal.

Write down everything you want to HAVE.

It might be simple stuff. It might be mega-crazy stuff; write it all down. Write it down. Write it down. Talk about it with *anyone you trust* who respects you and your desires.

- What do you want to have?
- How do you feel writing it down?
- How do you imagine feeling when it's yours?
- What is having it going to allow you to do?
- Will you be able to do more good in the world if you have this?

- Will you be able to help more people if you have this?

Now that you have your list, revisit it often. The fun is that your Be.Do.Have is never done. You can change, add, or delete. Most of all, have fun! Write what you want to Be.Do.Have into existence. I know I have.

By expressing gratitude for what I already have and consistently journaling about what I'd like to Be.Do.Have, I have written our dream life into existence. Who knows? Maybe as you're reading this, I'm already a New York Times Best Selling Author living in our family beach home sitting on the patio while Chris grills my favorite kebabs and I open my favorite wine before we listen to the boys tell us all about the adventures of their day and Aunt Pat and Uncle Mike are in town for a visit!

Your Jelly

*"Your time is limited, so don't waste it living someone else's life.
... have the courage to follow your heart and intuition."*
Steve Jobs

*J = the jelly represents your "Joy"
and is the specific area of your
excitement or expertise that you want
to package and sell to people.*

Finding Your Joy

Tamsen: It was about 3:30 am and I'd just tagged out
with Chris who was sleeping on the couch. Tad, our
youngest son, has reflux and so has a difficult time
sleeping and one of us *(99% of the time Chris)* sleeps on
the couch so we can hear him. I'd been up for about an
hour crying. A mother I don't even know but whom
I'm loosely connected with through different
friendships had gone for a walk the day before and was
hit by a car. She was banged up but her five-month-old
son was killed.

A few months ago a dear law school friend's son died
in his sleep just shy of his second birthday and only

months before his family welcomed his new baby sister. Another friend of a friend lost her daughter who was only four years old and then gave birth to her son the next morning.

"Change the world." "Live the life you love." "Find your joy." aren't clichés in our world. We know how quickly life can change and it's why we will talk about *Easy As PB&J* every single day of our lives. Living BIG in the mini moments of life is what we all have.

You've learned about finding what your peanut butter is made out of, how to uncover your ideal day, and what you'd like to Be.Do.Have. Now, it's time to release your jelly -- your JOY, the specific area of your excitement or expertise that you want to package and sell to people. A day-to-day way of living surrounded by carefree, cheerful, and delightful moments that leaves you satisfied and fulfilled.

We'll only ever encourage you to make PB&J products that bring you extreme happiness--JOY! Why would you make anything else? The new way of working, of adding PB&J to your life is based on tapping into those areas of you that make you smile and fuel your soul.

How do you know what your JOY is?

What if you use the wrong jelly? There really isn't a "wrong" jelly but as Gay Hendricks says in his international best seller *The Big Leap*, "Life is at its best when love, money, and creativity are growing in harmony." This is the level of happiness -- of JOY that we're after.

You might need to go through a couple different recipes to find your ultimate joy. My own joy journey took five years. But that's why we're here with you right now. To give you the opportunity to have your own thirty-seven minute experience like Chris did and save you from the five-year adventure I needed to take.

Snack Time: Find Your Joy

We have four different ways that you can explore to find your JOY. Try the one that feels best to you. Try another one a different day. The results all lead to the same place – helping you identify what really lights you up!

(1) Rearview mirror

(2) Your phone

(3) Start making a PB&J

(4) Make 20, one-minute videos

Rearview Mirror

Tamsen: The rearview mirror exercise that we worked through earlier also works really well to help you discover those moments in your life where you felt light, excited, time flew by, and your face hurt from smiling too much.

- What are some of your happiest memories? Good clues are when you were smiling, in a good mood, feeling lighthearted, and a sense of being carefree.
- What were you doing?
- Who were you with?
- What else can you recreate surrounding these moments?

Bringing the happy memories into the recipe of your PB&J. J is all about the area of excitement and expertise that you WANT to sell to someone else. Personally, I remember singing to myself as I organized all my dolls when I wasn't even yet five years old. Thinking back to those carefree moments when I was untroubled and simply organizing helped me tap into one of the layers of what brings me JOY.

Your Phone
Tamsen: I know it's not more than twelve inches away from you right now. Open up your pictures and take a look at them.

- What are you taking pictures of consistently?
- Which pictures make you smile?
- Where are you?
- What are you doing?
- Who are you with?

"A picture is worth a thousand words" refers to the notion that a complex idea can be conveyed with just a single still image and dates back to the early nineteen hundreds when it appeared in early advertisements by Fred. R. Barnard. There is a reason that Instagram® is powerful and was purchased by Facebook® in 2012 for $1 billion. One BILLION dollars! Pictures aren't only worth a thousand words, they're worth a BILLION dollars.

You can peek at our Instagram account @vacationinglife and see for yourself--Can you tell what makes us smile? Can you tell what we enjoy each day? Who do we love spending time with? I think you'll figure it out very quickly!

Start Making a PB&J

Chris: The key is to start. Just start. So often, we get hung up on every excuse to not start. Starting begins the journey.

Earlier, you had a chance to take a look at my real life PB&J story. I, *Mr. Skeptical himself,* after months of prodding, finally had an idea. I took my first "AHA" idea of what I could use to take through the PB&J system and I ran with it. It was awesome. In that short amount of time, just thirty-seven minutes, I was able to change the way I thought about work and how amazing it felt to know I could take what I knew and create something amazing to help others in the world. My mindset shifted in a way that was empowering. The game had just changed.

That life changing thirty-seven minutes happened in early June of 2016. I was so excited that I dove right in and began creating the lessons for my first PB&J on helping students create classroom presentations. At the same time, I also began using my new mindset *in other ways*. I began taking notes on other areas of interest. One in particular was being a dad and all the adventures that go along with that journey. I entitled the Evernote notebook, "You Get to Wipe a Poopy Butt" (*based on a song we sing in our house when we discover a "deuce" in a diaper*). It's basically a collection of stories related to my experiences since becoming a dad in 2011. When I write these stories, I laugh, I cry, I remember and I can't wait to live more adventures. My goal is to share my stories with new dads and dads who just found out they are going to be a dad for the first time. I love writing about being a dad!

In the middle of August of 2016, two months after going through the PB&J system, I realized that my presentation PB&J was *A product*, but it was not *THE product*. The real PB&J product I had been working on that I enJOYed above all else was, "You Get to Wipe a Poopy Butt". I just smile when I read that, it cracks me up that I am going to put a book out there with that title. I love it, it brings me joy and I know I would have bought it if I was a new dad, or Tamsen would have bought it for me. I am my target audience. I can't wait to write more entries. I can't wait to re-read what I wrote. I can't wait to get it out there to see what happens. THAT is a PB&J that I am meant to create.

So, how didn't I see the *right* PB&J *right out* of the gates? That really doesn't matter. What matters is getting started. Once you get started, you begin a transformational journey that allows you to open up all sorts of new ways to create, create and create some more. That's been a huge part of my adventure thus far. It's not wrong to create. Keep doing it. What you create should make you feel alive. What you create should wake you up in the middle of the night because you have a new idea. What you create should add to your life, not take away from it. In a little over two months, I learned not only can I create, I can create things that bring me joy and make a difference in the lives of others.

Just get started. Once you start, you'll be amazed how many ideas begin to flow.

Don't be afraid to set one PB&J aside if you find that your JOY lies somewhere else. That is the entire reason we wrote this book -- to help every one of us find what we love, share it with the world, and make money doing it.

Tag, you're it. Get started.

Make Twenty, One-Minute Videos

Tamsen: Unconventional? Absolutely! My dear friend Holly Gillen offers a fun online challenge-- #1min1take-- and I participate in it frequently. During my first time through the challenge, I started wandering around the house while the boys were napping and making quick videos on all kinds of *what I thought was random* stuff. Boy was I wrong!

When I looked through the playlist of what I'd made I saw immediately that what brings me joy - creating time and ideas and keeping them all safe. In less than an hour, my JOY crystallized because I naturally filmed what was easy for me and what I enjoyed sharing with others.

- Set a timer for one hour.
- Make twenty, one-minute videos.

- Upload them to YouTube (*keep them private if you want*)
- Look at what you recorded.

Ask yourself these questions:
- What did you talk about?
- What did you show "people"?
- How did you feel?
- Did you make videos that surprised you? If yes, how?

It really comes down to this: What do you want to be known for? Make that.

Tamsen: When I opened my law business, I thought my joy was found in helping people with their estate planning but when I heard this question, "What do you want to be known for?" My first thought was miles away from protecting people's money and property. This wasn't an easy question for me to answer right away. I had to let it rumble around inside me for a few weeks. I can't really say if I'd truly thought about being known for something.

As a mother to Kip and Tad, I know what I want to be known for. I want to be known for giving every single person the opportunity to discover his or her PB&J just like I did for Chris. To use my gifts and talents for bringing their genius, their excitement, all that is them to the surface and then walking right next to them to use those talents to change the trajectory of their lives. Now my mission is *Easy As PB&J*.

Snack Time: Choosing a Winner

Go through these questions for each area that you discovered in the *Snack Time: Find Your Joy* above that brings you happiness.

What is an area of your life and or knowledge that brings you JOY?

- How do you feel about this area?
- What's your experience with it?
- What could you teach other people about this area?
- Does it excite you?
- Does it provide extreme value?
- Give this area an overall JOY score. [1=lowest, 10=highest]

Do you have a clear winner?

If yes, then that should be your first PB&J product!

What if you don't have a clear winner? Chris didn't his first time through. He was looking at four entries all with a JOY score of 10. Did he stop? No, he didn't, he simply needed to dig a bit deeper by identifying the *extreme value* he could provide for his buyers.

Tie Breaker: Extreme Value

Extreme value provides maximum, exceptional, and extraordinary usefulness, benefit, and help to your buyers in a specific area in their lives based on what brings you JOY.

You only want to make PB&J product that excites you and brings the unexpected smile to your face and one that matters to your buyers. Products that matter provide extreme value in one of the following ways.

- How is the PB&J product that you're evaluating useful, functional, practical, or even convenient?
- How does it provide a benefit or a gain to your buyers?
- What does your product help your buyers do? Either by providing assistance, support, or guidance for them where they need you.
- What is exceptional, unusual, uncommon, or atypical about the product you're thinking about making?

- What is extraordinary, remarkable, amazing, or incredible about this PB&J?

Now you should have a clear winner on the area that excites you most and you're happy to start making into your PB&J.

Real Life PB&J Story: Fitness Coach & Yoga Teacher

The most important thing to know about the PB&J system is that it's simple.

Before reading *Easy As PB&J*, I was thinking on too large a scale and thinking I had to squeeze ALL of my ideas into one or two mega products. After reading it and observing the process I saw how to break down a larger idea into smaller pieces. It was eye-opening to see how ONE slice of information at a time can be just as effective to getting your overall mission across to the people you're trying to help. Like how Chris broke down starting as a "teacher" and going through the process to boil it down to Handraisers – helping kids build confidence for their presentations.

Easy As PB&J helped shift my vision to help me see that I can make very specific smaller courses within a larger structure of my main brand. I already have a 21-day workout program focused on transforming your mind in order to transform your body, as well as a new yoga-inspired workout coming out soon.

This book helped me see that I can create programs to help people within even more specific areas: meditations on positive body image, how to go from knees to full position in a push-up and have that variety of courses live under one umbrella.

I will definitely use the PB&J Course Design system to create my next product because it helps me channel my creative mind and provides me the structure to get from idea to action!

I'm also getting my husband to read *Easy As PB&J* because I know he has a ton of PB&J ready to show the world!

Elyse Sparkes, Fitness Coach & Yoga Trainer | elysesparkes.com

Your Bread

B = the bread represents your "Buyers." The people you will share your areas of excitement or expertise with while they pay you for the value you've added to their life.

Your Brand

Tamsen: Right now I'm sitting at my IKEA® desk working on my iMac® sipping coffee out of my Kajabi® mug with a Tupperware® cup full of water also right within reach. I have my Day Designer® planner open and my Staedler® markers open and ready to write down my next thought.

That's six brands and I didn't move a muscle! I could've listed another fifty brands surrounding me right now but I think you get the idea. Everything about us: our personality, our appearance, our mannerisms, our [everything] makes up our brand. People buy brands every single day. We know this fact. What we we don't know and honestly, are rarely taught is that *we are brands*. When I read the international best-seller by Tom Peters, *Brand You*, how I saw myself forever changed:

Regardless of age, regardless of position, regardless of the business we happen to be in, all of us need to understand the importance of branding. We are CEOs of our own companies: Me, Inc. To be in business today, our most important job is to be head marketer for the brand called You.

Why didn't I learn this in junior high, high school, college, or graduate school? Suddenly thoughts were flooding my mind and speeding through my rearview mirror.

- When I worked at a telemarketing company in high school - I was a brand.
- When I worked as a teaching assistant in college - I was a brand.
- When I worked at a bagel store, after tanking my planned out career in medicine - I was a brand.
- When I built a figure skating program of four hundred families in eighteen months - I was a brand.
- When I worked in collegiate trademark licensing - I was a brand.
- Now, as I sit here with you - I am a brand.

YOU are a brand. You've always been a brand. You're not an employee -- you're a brand that a buyer (*aka your employer*) buys every time he or she gives you a paycheck. So if you're wondering as you're reading this book whether anyone will buy what you have, ask yourself: are you receiving a paycheck? Have you ever received a paycheck?

If you answer yes to either of those questions, then *you already* have buyers. If you sold lemonade on the edge of your driveway, you had a buyer. The fear or apprehension you feel isn't a fear of "Will anyone buy what I'm making?" because they already are. The fear is "Do I have the courage to step out and *find new buyers* for what brings me joy?"

Mislabeled

Tamsen: I often receive mail addressed to "Mr. Tamsen Horton" and I immediately know to toss it into the trash. The sender used the wrong label and obviously doesn't know me or have a connection to me. If they did they would use the correct label "Mrs. Tamsen Horton."

I'd like to propose that while "employee" and "employer" are commonplace in the traditional work system, they are the *wrong* labels. They serve to identify the hierarchy of power but don't accurately portray the relationship of the transaction. "Maker" and "buyer" are the correct labels. "You, as the CEO of Me, Inc." as

Tom Peters teaches are the brand that is *making* what your employer, the buyer, is buying.

Just like I quickly rid myself of junk mail when I see the wrong label, when you remove the "employee" label and replace it with "maker" suddenly you see the tremendous financial value you hold as a creator of products and services that your "employer" buyer is willing to purchase.

A feeling of power and control is built-in to being a maker. That's what you are! You are a maker.

Every single time you receive a paycheck, you are the maker and the person or company paying you is the buyer. The company is buying your knowledge, enthusiasm, promptness, manners, and skills. Even if you view yourself as a cog in a large wheel, you are *making* something of value for the person or company paying you. Otherwise, they wouldn't pay you. They wouldn't buy "You, as the CEO of Me, Inc."

You are a maker and your boss is your buyer. You are *already* making products. They might not be PB&J products yet but you're definitely already well trained in making (*aka working*). Right now in this quiet moment, take a deep breath and say to yourself, "I am a maker and my boss is my buyer. I already have a buyer."

- If you can sell to one buyer why couldn't you sell to another?
- Why couldn't you sell something different (*if you wanted to*)?
- Why couldn't you branch out and leverage what you already know -- that's why we wrote this book for you.

The world is full of your buyers! And now we're going to find them.

Snack Time: Today, who is buying what you are making?

Tamsen: Let's take a few moments to take inventory of your current buyer(s) and see what qualities are a good fit for you and where you might want to change things up.

- As of today, how are you receiving payments for your knowledge, skills, etc.?
- What is the buyer's name (aka your boss or employer) on the checks that you receive?
- How long has this person or company been buying your services?
- How do you feel about this buyer?
- Are you happy and full of gratitude when you interact with your buyer?
- How do you feel when you go to work?

- How do you feel throughout the day?
- Do you feel that your buyer respects and appreciates the value you are providing to them? (after all, they are buying what you are selling)

Let's say you love your buyer - awesome! When I was working in collegiate trademark licensing, I worked in an *ideal place* with amazing people. I loved my buyers (aka my boss), but I craved more. I *had* to become a lawyer to satisfy the *more* that was bubbling up inside of me.

Chris loves his buyers and he has multiple layers involved: the taxpayers that provide the funds for our public school district, and the school district that buys his amazing services each year and finally, the kids who are buying into the lessons he is selling. But as you've seen after he experienced the PB&J system for himself he wanted to add new buyers, different buyers, to his life.

New Buyers Please
On the other hand, maybe you don't particularly like or care for your current buyer. We've both had plenty of jobs that frustrated us, sucked the life out of us— you know the ones where it takes every ounce of energy, patience, and biting of the tongue just to make it through the day. When we were in those situations we

felt like we didn't have a choice. That we needed to be thankful we had a job and just suck it up and deal with it. Little did we know that we had chosen that frustrating boss in a million different little ways.

Yes, we chose those life-sucking jobs. Just like *you chose* your current buyer. Plain and simple. Love them or not, you chose them. Whatever you wrote, said, called, clicked, etc. that persuaded your buyer to hire you is how you chose the situation that you are currently living. And as is life if you want different experiences, you simply need to make new choices.

- Did you send in a resume?
- Did you respond to a help wanted ad?
- Did you ask someone to recommend you?

As you're making your PB&J product you need buyers otherwise you'll be sitting on a whole lot of great products and making no money. But you don't want just any buyer, you want to get your PB&J into the hands of the exact people who are going to love giving you their hard-earned money. When you find the sweet spot of sharing what you know with exactly the people that you really enjoy -- it's simply one of the best treasures in life!

Snack Time: Who are your favorite people?

> *B = the bread represents your "Buyers." The people you will share your areas of excitement or expertise with while they pay you for the value you've added to their life.*

Tamsen: We'd be willing to bet that you already have a surplus of ideal paying customers and in a few minutes, you'll have all their names written down. In your journal, write down all the names that come to mind as you think through these questions.

Who do you ...

- Love having dinner with?
- Enjoy going out for drinks with?
- Laugh out loud when you read their social media updates?
- Simple adore?
- Really enjoy working with?
- Love talking with?
- Love spending time with?

Now that you've written these names down, would you please introduce me to them? If you were sitting across from me at a cafe, how would you describe these people that matter to you? What would you tell me about the person you simply adore?

- Where do they live?
- How many kids do they have?
- Do they have kids?
- Where do they work?
- Do they enjoy what they do for work?
- Are there any similarities in their stories?
- How are they different?
- How are you connected with them?
- How long have they been in your life?
- Where do they shop? What do they buy?
- What's the biggest concern, problem, or source of stress in their life right now?

Again, do you see similarities and differences in them? What do you see? The purpose of this exercise is to start to create your ideal paying customer profile. When you know your buyer and understand the lives they are currently leading, then it becomes easy to see how your PB&J fits into their life.

Ideal Paying Customers

As you're looking over your answers, are there any people that you would consider your perfect or ideal buyer? Who is the person or people that you'd be over-the-moon excited if they purchased one of your PB&J products?

What specifically makes this person ideal for you? This is the perfect time to use your pen to underline or circle the parts of the stories that make this person right for you as a potential buyer.

If you find yourself saying, "Tamsen, no one that I've listed is a good buyer for me. These are my friends, but they're not going to buy my stuff."

I'd say you're wrong but for the sake of discussion let's say you're right -- not a single friend is going to buy your PB&J. However, you likely want your buyer to share similar qualities to the people that you enjoy being around.

So let's put our thinking caps on, what is missing? Why isn't ONE of the names you've listed making the list as an ideal paying customer?

Sharing v. Selling

Tamsen: The subtitle of this book is "*Share* what you know" for a reason. It's not "*Sell* what you know."

If the idea of needing to "sell" freaks you out, I'd like to offer you this mindset shift. Instead of seeing yourself as a salesperson, think of yourself as a teacher. As a teacher, your role is to simply teach your buyers what you know. You made a PB&J to help them achieve a desired result or solve a problem in their lives and now you share that excitement or expertise with them.

You're not selling to them. You are teaching them and when you adopt a teaching mindset the pressure to close the sale goes away.

Snack Time: Your "Secret" Bread Recipe

Tamsen: I like to call this your secret bread recipe. If you've ever been to a bakery, you know that they typically have no less than a dozen different types of bread on display. Why is that? Aren't they all simply loaves of bread? I know silly question - of course, each loaf is different! It's the differences that draw us into the bakery!

As you answer each of these questions, each answer is simply one of the ingredients that make up your bread.

> *B = the bread represents your "Buyers." The people you will share your areas of excitement or expertise with while they pay you for the value you've added to their life.*

Every single person and company that sells anything (even if they give it away for free) knows who his or her buyers are. Just for a moment think about the differences between Apple® and Wal-Mart® or Panera® and McDonald's®.

Every day these companies are thinking about and analyzing their buyers and making millions of decisions to make the best PB&J product that they can so people will keep buying.

This is one place where we simply had to restrain ourselves and not put all the information we have about buyers in the book. If you want more information on this topic you'll find it in the multimedia experience. (bit.ly/pbjmultimedia)

- How is your buyer spending their time when they are working?
- Are they an employee?
- Are they paid hourly or do they receive a salary?
- Do they own their own business?
- How is your buyer spending their free time?
- If you had to tell me a bit about your buyer, what would you say?
- For instance, she's a work-at-home mom with two little kids who enjoys being a mom and also using her skill set and college degree to create an income stream for her family.
- What does your buyer stress about?

- Is it not having enough money at the end of the month, or how they'll pay for college, or simply how to make a prize-worthy pie?
- Stress is stress and we all have it in varying degrees.
- What is your buyer already buying?
- What did they buy today?
- What did they buy in the last week, the last month, the last year?
- What do they return?
- What can't they live without?

Each of these questions is helping you focus on how to talk about your PB&J, where to spend your time as you start sharing your PB&J, and most of all finding the places where you can intersect your buyers world in meaningful ways. When you know the life stories about your buyers, then you can find ways to connect with them and share your PB&J.

One example that we can share directly related to this book is that our ideal customer and reader is someone who hangs out in coffee shops. Over the years we've developed relationships with a couple of our favorite coffee shops and are able to leave copies of our book for their customers. We also created a really cool FUNdraising program where displaying our books is a win-win for the business. It is this process of learning to describe your buyers that allows you to find the ideal places for your PB&J products.

- A reader gets access to a book they might not otherwise read.
- The business gets access to our FUNdraising program.
- We are able to spread our PB&J message in ways that bring us JOY!

Real Life PB&J Story: Website Designer

The most important thing you need to know about the PB&J system is it's super simple and quick and it's stinking genius!

Before using the PB&J Course Design system I was spinning my wheels. I knew I had a group programme inside of me but had no idea of what it was or how it could look. Tamsen's PB&J system brought what I knew was lurking around under the surface right out in front of my eyes. I felt a bit silly for not being able to see it before!

All results of taking PB&J pointed to being able to help those who needed to just get started already with a website that worked for them and their biz. As a result, I created … "A Website that WORKS!" A six-week online group coaching programme where I walk participants through everything they need to do ahead of launching a website. Then at the end, my company gives them an actual website and all the tutorials they need in order to pop their content in and LAUNCH to the world!

This six-week program - the idea that came out of my first run through of PB&J Course Design went on to create over $24,000 in income through its BETA launch. Now I'm gearing up for a bigger release and who knows where this could take me. PB&J has allowed me to find my path to freedom from my desk, more time with my family, and a lifestyle I thought was years and years away.

If you asked me if I'd keep using the PB&J method to create my next product my answer is -- Abso-freakin-LUTEly! Crystal clarity and ideas with substance have been emerging like wildfire. There's no stemming this tide.

Laura Husson, Founder and Director at Husson Media Ltd | laurahusson.com

PB&J System

"Creativity is intelligence having fun."
Albert Einstein

Why It's Called PB&J

Tamsen: When I was a law professor I needed to teach future lawyers the importance of providing clear instructions in a way that *anyone* could understand. Always one inspired to keep learning fun, I had two students come to the front of the room. Laid out in front of them were a loaf of bread, a jar of peanut butter and jelly, a knife, a plate, and a blindfold. One student put the blindfold on and the other student had to give the instructions on how to assemble the peanut butter and jelly sandwich.

As you might imagine there were plenty of laughs when the instructions were *less than* clear. The blindfolded person had to be told which direction to move his hands, how far away the item was, and exactly what to do with each ingredient.

There was jelly dropped on the floor and peanut butter smeared on a hand but in the end *the lesson was engraved* on their brains: order matters and clearly explain each step.

When you're making a PB&J product you need to tell your buyers every single step: teach them exactly how you would teach someone to make a peanut butter and jelly sandwich. This is why this system is called PB&J. *(The first time I taught this publicly online it was called "Design an e-course in under an hour" -- PB&J Course Design is so much better!)*

What you may find is that often it's hard to teach someone else how to do what you know so well; but if you can, and you do it well, then you become a PB&J master.

First A Plate

If you were making a *real* peanut butter and jelly sandwich, you'd need a plate to put it on. As you're making your digital PB&J you need a place, a system, to brainstorm, organize, create and ultimately sell your PB&J.

We're going to give you a few different ideas but you know yourself best. Use the system that's right for you, be open to some new ideas, but most of all let's make this PB&J!

Mind mapping

Tamsen: My ultimate and go-to tool for everything I do is mind mapping. As best-selling author Michael Michalko describes this tool in his book *Thinkertoys*,

> *"Mapping presents information organized in the way you think. It displays the way your mind works, complete with patterns and interrelationships, and has an amazing capacity to convey precise information."*

If you've never seen a mind map then quickly Google "mind map" and you'll see an array of images and the sheer variety of ways that you can display information using mind-mapping techniques.

Chris and I use digital mind maps as the starting point whenever we are creating PB&J products. We highly recommend Mindmeister.com because this single tool allows us to capture the ideas, store them, create them, and then also have the map serve as an avenue to make our money.

Paper Notebooks

I'm giving you the benefit of my 20/20 hindsight ... find a notebook you love and order five of them. Having the same notebook makes storage and creating a system very easy. Personally, I use the Mead® Academie™ Sketch Book (9 in x 6 in). I know the value of handwriting ideas and so I keep paper nearby at all times. You'll likely use paper for capturing and organizing ideas and then move over to your computer to do the actual creating. After all, your PB&J is a digital product.

Electronic Notebooks

Evernote® and Google® Drive are our go-to tools for our digital content. In either tool, we can create notebooks and folders to keep the information organized. When I'm making a PB&J product, after I've mapped out the content with a mind map then I create a notebook in Evernote and a note for each of the PB&J system pieces.

Whiteboards

If a scientist ever invents whiteboard paint I'm repainting my office immediately! We have four whiteboards hung throughout our home to capture ideas as they happen. In our family office, the whiteboard is displayed as a piece of artwork. The ideas we've written on it definitely rival the sales of famous artists' paintings.

Sticky notes

Gotta love a good sticky note and thank goodness Arthur Fry saw the benefit in taking a fellow colleague's accidental mistake and creating what we all know as the Post-it® note. I always have post-it notes nearby. The beauty of this as a PB&J tool is that you can stick them anywhere without inflicting damage.

The Pieces

Tamsen: As you've read the Real Life PB&J Stories, the genius of this system is its simplicity. There's a reason that the actual system is the shortest part of the book - it's easy to implement. It's far harder to get our mindset lined up with the idea that we can take what we know, share it, and make money doing it.

> *"The problem with so many of us is that we underestimate the power of simplicity."*
> *Robert Stuberg*

These are the pieces that make up the PB&J system and we will take each one individually:

- The INTRODUCTION
- The LEARNING TARGETS which are what you want your buyer to know how to do when they complete your product.
- BONUS MATERIALS that are complementary resources and or information that enhance your buyer's experience.

That's it.

When your curiosity strikes and you'd like to see examples of actual PB&J products, please use the multimedia experience. (bit.ly/pbjmultimedia)

Learning Targets

First of all, *what* is the PB&J that you are going to make?

> *PB&J = the sandwich and represents the digital product you can make to sell by packaging the areas of excitement and expertise you already have.*

The first pieces of the PB&J system that you are going to create are your learning targets. The learning targets are what you want your buyer to be able to do, learn, navigate, etc. after they purchase your PB&J.

The learning targets support the purpose of your PB&J.

For example, our purpose in this book was to share with you how you can take what you know, share it with other people and make money doing it.

The learning targets that supported this purpose were that we wanted our reader to

1. Understand how the current system of work is incomplete and broken.
2. Understand what their peanut butter is.
3. Understand what their jelly is.
4. Understand what their bread is.
5. Make their first PB&J product.

Snack Time: Making Your Learning Targets

First, what is the *purpose* of your PB&J? What is the reason you are making your PB&J product?

Second, what are three things you want your buyer to be able to do as a result of using your PB&J product? These are your learning targets. *A good rule of thumb when making your first PB&J product is that three learning targets are proportional to a $100 product. I'll be showing you an example below that if put together would make a great $100 PB&J product.*

1. My buyer will be able to do this, understand this, learn this, build this, etc.
2. My buyer will be able to do this, understand this, learn this, build this, etc.
3. My buyer will be able to do this, understand this, learn this, build this, etc.

Now, please be kind to yourself as you're laying out your learning targets - you are likely to change your mind more than a few times, and rarely do the learning targets come out in order. You should be prepared to adjust what you write frequently! That's the number one reason why I use and only recommend using a mind map to build your PB&J product. It's the only way to see the big picture, the tiny details, and move any idea around as you gain clarity.

Under each learning target answer these three questions:

1. Why does your buyer need to do this, understand this, learn this, build this, etc.?
2. What are three positive results when your buyer achieves what you listed in question 1 above?
3. How to make it happen? *This is the action step and where you'll provide your buyer the step-by-step instruction they need to accomplish question 1 and achieve the results of question 2.*

Here is an *example* of a completed learning target:

Learning target [number]: I want my buyer to be able to do [this].

1. My buyer needs to know how to do [this] because [result desired]

2. Three specific positives that are a natural result/consequence of knowing how to do [this] are ...

3. Here are the step-by-step instructions on how my buyer can achieve [result desired] step 1, step 2, etc. (*How does your buyer get from where they are now to where they want to be?*)

Easy As PB&J was simply a series of this learning target pattern repeated and then delivered as an online course, a book, and lecture series.

Illustration: Sewing a Custom Pillowcase

Let's take a simple illustration - learning how to sew a custom pillowcase and walk through step-by-step how this system creates the PB&J product. Then when you're ready to make your PB&J, simply substitute out the sewing example for your own content.

As the resident expert on sewing pillowcases (*just for the next few pages*), your role is to make learning how to sew a custom pillowcase easier for your buyer. A buyer that paid you $100 to learn this skill from you -- your PB&J product.

Step 1: Identify the Purpose of Your PB&J Product
The purpose of my PB&J product is to help my buyer sew beautiful, customized pillowcases.

Step 2: Use the Learning Target Template
You do this by answering the learning target questions
listed above.

Learning target 1: I want my buyer to know how to
operate his or her sewing machine.

- *[answer to question 1]* My buyer ***needs to know
  how to*** operate his or her sewing machine
  because they will have a difficult time sewing a
  pillowcase by hand.

- **[answer to question 2]***Three positive results*
  that my buyer will achieve by knowing how to
  operate his or her sewing machine are:
    1. A positive result is that my buyer will
       know how to thread the needle on the
       sewing machine, so he or she can
       change the thread color.
    2. A positive result is that my buyer will
       know how to change the bobbin, so he
       or she can rethread it and also change
       the color of thread.
    3. A positive result is that my buyer will
       know how to switch the settings
       between different stitches.

- *[answer to question 3]* ***The steps my buyer needs
  to take*** to learn how to operate his or her
  sewing machine are:

- Step 1 - *Here is where you need to tell your buyer exactly the steps they need to take to operate the sewing machine. You are the expert and it is your job to teach your buyer the steps they need to take.*
- Step 2
- Step 3
- Step ... *continue teaching all the steps necessary to operate the sewing machine.*

Step 3: Repeat Step 2 for Each Learning Target

When you've done this you will have three learning targets that contain the content necessary to support your purpose: *helping your buyer learn how to sew a custom pillowcase.*

Order Matters

As the expert, your role is to identify for your buyers when they MUST do steps in a certain order and when they have a choice.

For instance, when my students were helping each other make the peanut butter and jelly sandwich in class, they could choose whether they wanted to work with the peanut butter or the jelly first. But they couldn't choose whether they wanted to take the bread out of its bag. They had to take the bread out of the bag first, or they wouldn't have a place for the peanut butter or jelly to go.

These specific instructions and their organization determine why your buyer is willing to pay you. You are making their life easier; helping them learn a new skill, avoid a difficult experience, or any other number of positive outcomes.

Bonus Materials: Buy 1, Get 2 Free!

Tamsen: As you're making your PB&J product, are there complementary areas that you could create "bonus materials" for? After all, everyone loves a great bonus!

The key word being a *GREAT* bonus. You want to make sure that what you're offering to your buyers makes sense and creates a feeling of excitement for your buyers. I've personally witnessed people spending hours trying to explain how to make a great bonus when in reality it boils down to answering two really simple questions:

- What learning target is the bonus tied to?
- Why is the bonus content NOT already included in the learning target that it's tied to?

You're welcome. It really is that simple!

Now, if you're going to make your own bonus content, all you need to do is follow the same learning target recipe and you're done.

1. Why do my buyers need to know this?
2. What are three specific positives my buyer can achieve with this bonus material?
3. How to make it happen (action)?

If you have identified an area of bonus content that isn't your zone of genius, then use someone that is. Invite the expert to share their zone of genius with your community and create a win-win situation for everyone.

Don't be afraid to give your guest expert your PB&J system. As someone who is frequently asked to provide content surrounding my areas of expertise: creating time ideas and keeping them all safe, I would welcome an invitation where there is a template as simple as this one to follow.

The Introduction

Tamsen: While the introduction is the first part of your buyer's experience. It is the final piece that you make. Why? Inside your introductory content you are going to provide a summary of what your buyer can expect and you don't want to make the summary until you know you've placed everything in the best order. You'll see that there are two main categories that make up the introduction: start here and welcome.

How Much Detail Does the Introduction Need?

The amount and detail you need as part of the introduction of your PB&J depend entirely on the format that you've chosen for your product.

- A simple pdf download probably doesn't need much more than a paragraph.
- A series of audio recordings might only need a brief introduction on the first audio.
- A mini-course delivered online might need to have a video showing the buyer how to interact with the content.

We're going to walk you through the different pieces that make up the content of the "introduction" but please visit the multimedia experience to see the examples we've provided.

The Start Here Portion of the Introduction

Once you've created your learning targets, then you have the roadmap of how you're going to teach your buyers your PB&J. The "start here" material is your opportunity to share with your buyers exactly where you're going to take them.

For example, "In this product, you're going to learn (1), (2), and (3)." You are the expert in this area (*it's why you made the PB&J!*) so you'll know how simple or detailed your *start here* instructions need to be for your buyers.

As you're providing the summary or the roadmap for your buyers, can you provide them with a finished example or two? You've definitely seen this in the multimedia experience (bit.ly/pbjmultimedia) where we shared examples of what a finished PB&J product might look like.

How many examples do you need? Well, imagine you are looking at a recipe book. Some recipe books have a picture for each recipe, and others might have one picture for a whole section. What is going to help your buyer visualize their result the best?

The Welcome Portion of the Introduction

Maximize that first impression with your buyers, and welcome them to your product in a meaningful and clear way.

Since there are limitless ways to create a PB&J, you'll need to look at the type of PB&J that you made and decide what is the best way to start your relationship with them. Here are some ideas to help you get started.

Provide a Tour

Think about each time you've gone to visit a friend at their home for the first time - did you immediately know the layout of their home? Probably not. You needed them to give you a quick "orientation tour" so you'd know where the bathroom was, the kitchen, where they'd like you to hang your coat, etc.

The PB&J that you are creating might require you to take your buyer on a quick "orientation tour." For example, most of the PB&J products that we create are online multimedia experiences and it's really important for us to walk our buyers through where to find what they need. If you sign up for the FREE PB&J Course Design™ Sampler found in the multimedia experience, the first information that you'll see is a welcome video.

List of Essential Tools

To make cupcakes, you need a cupcake pan. To sew, you need a sewing machine.

For what you are teaching your buyers to do, are there any tools that they MUST have to accomplish what you are guiding them through? If yes, you need to let them know that.

For PB&J Course Design™ there are four essential tools and I make sure to share that with my community. As an example, to make a PB&J you need a way to organize your content and an essential tool is something like Dropbox®, Evernote®, Google® Drive, or on their computer.

While there are essential tools, you probably have your personal favorites that you've figured out based on your years of personal and professional experience, and that is where you provide your recommended resources.

List of Recommended Resources

In addition to any essential tools your buyer needs, are there any resources that you've discovered along your journey that make life easier, faster, better, etc.?

One of the best ways you can serve your buyers is by providing them access to your "Little Black Book."

Don't be afraid of saying, "Here's the best tool for this." Your ideal buyers appreciate this honesty because you are saving them the headache of trying to sort through various options. I used to say, "here are three options you could use." Now, I say, "This is what works and it's all I recommend." When you know what works say it. People understand that they have options, what they want to know is what is going to get them the results they want in the easiest and best way possible.

Recently, we were visiting our favorite homebuilders during the spring Parade of Homes in our city and one woman commented on how beautiful the kitchen cabinets were. Our builder didn't skip a beat and said she'd give the woman her source. The look on the woman's face was priceless—utter shock that the builder would share that information with her – one of the thousand or so reasons that we respect this builder and will be using them to build our ideal home.

When you know the best resources, share them. Constantly talking about the really good people, products, and services is how you help mold the world into the place you want. Look no further than the story of Clint Harp, a custom furniture maker, who went from being flat broke with his wife and three children and in a little under nine months was featured alongside Chip and Joanna Gaines on their hit home renovation show *Fixer Upper*. Joanna loved Clint's work, she talked about it, and now Clint receives orders from all over the world for his work.

Your Turn

Tamsen: That's it, the entire PB&J system! It took me longer to type it out then it will take for you to make your PB&J product.

When you start, document your journey. Your future self will thank you. I had NO idea where our journey would take us when I had Chris go and sit on our porch with the laptop. Fortunately I listened to my gut and documented this entire process. Much like looking back through baby books, it's really fun and rewarding to see how our crazy PB&J life has played out.

Please share your journey with us. We love cheering and will gladly celebrate all your wins and help you through any struggles as you make your PB&J products. Tag us on social media @vacationinglife and @tamsenhorton

Our Wish For You

"Collaboration"

"Everyone wins."

"I have a talent and a story to share."

"I want to jump up and DO something!"

A world infused with these feelings, filling social media feeds, and inspiring family discussions, this is our wish for you.

To have you feeling inspired to take a talent, or a piece of knowledge, or simply a topic you're interested in and create a way to share that with other people and make money doing it. That's what we want for you.

Our wish is that you have all the freedom and time you want to spend in the way you want with the people you value, love, and respect most in life.

You'll never know Bo, but his wish was that every single person be safe and taken care of. You taking what you've read in *Easy As PB&J* and creating a life for you and your family that you LOVE living is something he'd be so proud of and is how we are able to honor his life.

Next Steps

What's most important to us is that you *see the incredible value that you have inside you.* You are a special person with unique talents and skills and we're so thankful to have spent this time with you sharing our PB&J with you.

We wrote this book for you so you would have the map you need to take action.

When you take action is entirely up to you. We hope that it is sooner rather than later because life is short and you deserve to have the best most amazing #vacationinglife ever! Starting today.

Option 1: Share Easy As PB&J with a friend

Making a PB&J and going through this experience is even better with friends. So send your closest friend this website address www.easyaspbj.com and invite them to join you and make their own PB&J!

Option 2: Start making your PB&J

We want you to experience the feelings of excitement, empowerment, and fulfillment that come from starting to make a PB&J product. We wrote this book as a map for you so you could *smoothly* navigate your way to exactly where you want to go. The entire PB&J Course Design system, the gourmet version, is the best way to make your PB&J and it's included in our Vacationing Life Community.

We'd love to give you a free month in our Vacationing Life Community. Come on in and see what it's like to surround yourself with other inspired individuals who are also working on creating their PB&J. Enter this coupon code: 1000STRONG on this page bit.ly/makemypbj

As Jim Rohn, entrepreneur, author, and mentor to Tony Robbins and Jack Canfield said, "You are the average of the five people you spend the most time with." The individuals and families of #vacationinglife are definitely ones you want to add to your average. Even if you feel like you're not quite ready to make a PB&J, come hang out with us. Let us encourage you and help you brainstorm ways to start cashing in on that ATM located between your ears.

Option 3: We don't have one
Your life intersected this book and us for a reason. From this moment on, you are never going to look at a peanut butter and jelly sandwich the same way! Just like when the explorers ventured into new worlds there was no turning back. The good news is not only has the

exploring been charted but also the boat is made, the staff is ready, and your first-class cabin is all ready.

When you're ready, we're here. We're not going anywhere and as our dear friend, pediatric dentist, and mother to three amazing kids said:

> *"PB&J is something you might not be able to use RIGHT now in life but the information will stick with you until you have your own "AHA" moment. You will then have the knowledge at your fingertips."*

Peanut Butter & Chocolate

"They go together like chocolate and peanut butter."
Paul Sagawa

Easy As PB&J + New Kajabi

At Halloween, as you quietly dig through your child's "haul", what are you secretly looking for? We're pretty sure it's the peanut butter cups because every parent we know admits to digging for the peanut butter cups! Including us! What is it about those little nuggets of chocolate and peanut butter that turns everyday law-abiding parents into sneaky little "thieves" after our children have gone to bed?

Simple. There's nothing quite like chocolate and peanut butter.

You've learned about "peanut butter" and it's time we told you about the chocolate that we've paired with our "peanut butter". Pairing is too mild – we've encased our PB&J in chocolate and we've found the best chocolate in the whole world.

Meet New Kajabi.

"New K-what? What the heck is New Kajabi?" Yes, we can hear your thoughts.

> **New Kajabi is a brilliant online system (technically an application) that we run our entire website and business from. It's our PB&J factory, distribution center, and bank.**

When you decide to sell your PB&J products you need certain tools to deliver your products and take payment. This is what New Kajabi does but it does so much more and that's why we talk about it all the time!

Now, if you are brand new to the idea of selling what you know online, then in the pages that follow we're going to briefly outline for you the technical aspects that go into selling your PB&J online. There are lots of moving pieces when you don't use New Kajabi and each one serves a specific and essential function. We're including this information because you need to know it exists, but you might not need to take action right now. Your number one focus is starting to make your PB&J.

Moving our entire business over to New Kajabi in November 2015 decreased our expenses by 46% and our "work" time by 87% and that's why we want to share our story with you.

Before New Kajabi entered the marketplace in November 2015, we spent months researching and comparing the different tools required to sell online. We'll walk you through each of those tools in the upcoming pages. The short story is it was very expensive, time-consuming, and stressful.

Our five-year experience in selling digital products has a silver lining. Had we not tried numerous other tools and spent thousands of dollars we wouldn't appreciate the solution that New Kajabi now provides and we wouldn't be able to help you like we can now.

Selling Digital Products

Tamsen: There are many ways that you can set up your PB&J distribution and buying experience for your buyers. Ultimately, all systems boil down to these key elements:

- Create a digital product. *This is your PB&J.*

- Upload the product onto a website.
- Set up a product delivery process so you can get your PB&J to your buyers.
- Set up a payment system so you can take money.
- Let your buyers know that you have a PB&J product available to purchase.

Every person selling online has a system that performs these tasks.

The Tools Required

Tamsen: As we lay out all the tools that are required, please know that we only use one tool, New Kajabi.

The reason that we chose to build our wealth legacy with New Kajabi is simply because after learning about what their product could do, we knew that they had built the best system for families like us that wanted to create a long-term strategy for cashing in on what's tucked away between our ears.

If you are a visual learner, we've also created a visual diagram of how the tools fit together that is available in the multimedia experience (bit.ly/pbjmultimedia).

The only tool outside of New Kajabi is GoDaddy.com when we purchase custom domain names. *New Kajabi doesn't sell domain registration.*

Ultimately, after much debate about whether to include this information within the book we decided that five years ago we wish we would've had a list like this. A list that told us exactly what we were going to need to sell our knowledge online and the approximate costs.

This list will save you time, money, and stress.

Custom Cars and PB&J

Imagine you're holding a beautiful catalogue from your favorite carmaker and now your task is to choose the model, the trim level, and have it delivered to your New York City apartment building parking garage.

One of Bo's (*Tamsen's cousin*) favorite things to do was to choose their family's new cars. He was very good at it and so in honor of him, we're going to teach you about selling online products using this illustration -- ordering and customizing a car.

Domain Name

This is your "parking spot" on the Internet, your website.
- Your domain name is identified by its URL.
- Common system: godaddy.com

- Pricing: Average $20 per domain address *with* privacy protection.

Hosting

When you park your car in New York City, you'll need to pay a parking garage for your reserved spot. This is what hosting is. You will pay a monthly or annual fee to a company to park your car (your website).

- Similar to a regular parking garage, there will be lots and lots of other cars parked in the other parking spots.
- Common system: Bluehost.com
- Pricing: Average $300 per year

Platform

This is where you choose the *basic* model and engine of the car (website), that you will park in your parking spot (hosting). We chose New Kajabi as the model and engine of our car (website).

- Once you have your domain name (parking spot) and hosting (parking garage) set up, then you can start customizing your car.
- Common systems: New Kajabi, Wordpress.org, Squarespace, Weebly, Teachable, Thinkific, and *probably no less than a thousand others.*
- Pricing: Free -- $100+ per month

Security

Security is your insurance policy that covers full replacement coverage for your website (car).

- Let's say hackers decide to completely smash your website (car) one day by hacking it or sending you a virus.
- Your security system comes to your rescue by sending you an exact duplicate of your website (car) immediately.
- Security does this by automatically making backup copies of your website (car) so they're ready for just such an emergency.
- Common system: Back-up Buddy sold by ithemes.com
- Pricing: Average $50 per month

Spam Filter

You have to protect yourself from hackers smashing your car (website) and also from the spammers that want to cover your car (website) with millions of annoying bumper stickers (spam) when you're not looking. A spam filter keeps unwanted comments off your website (car).

- Think about a spam filter as the tool that gives your website (car) an amazing wax job making it impossible for bumper stickers (spam) to stick. Spam filters give your car the best wax job available.

- When the spammers try to plaster their annoying bumper stickers (unwanted comments) all over your blog (located on your website), the spam filter makes it so the bumper stickers can't stick.
- Common system: Akismet.com
- Pricing: Average $5 per month

Website theme

A website theme is what allows you to customize the model and engine of your car (website). Choosing if you'd like leather or fabric seats, the sports package, and what kind of wheels you'd like is what the website theme does.

For example New Kajabi has different themes to choose from and when we choose the format we like then we can change the colors, font, pictures, etc. This is how two different people using the same theme will have entirely different looking websites (cars).

- Common system: Depends on the platform you chose. To find themes for your platform (model and engine of car) type "[platform name] themes" into a search engine and you'll have a great place to start. For example before moving to New Kajabi our websites (cars) were on the Wordpress.org platform and we used

website themes from woothemes.com to customize the look of the website (car).
- Pricing: Average $50

Search Engine Optimization (SEO)

- We're giving you the "real person's guide to SEO" here -- SEO is basically the instantaneous results of a popularity contest you enter by typing into a search engine.
- The most popular cars (websites) show up on page one of Google®.
- People pay thousands of dollars to land on page one of Google and spend hours of time trying to do so. Please as you are starting to make your PB&J products save your time, energy, and money right now.
- Focus on making your PB&J products and getting your website (car) set up and then move onto SEO.
- Pricing: DO NOT pay anyone for SEO until you understand what you're doing! This is one area where people are routinely taken advantage of.

Blog

- A blog is an entry on your website (car) where you write about different areas of interest related to your PB&J products.

- A good place to start blogging is writing one article a month. You can even choose to make a video instead and that is called vlogging.
- Common system: A blog is included in your website (car) and customized with your website theme
- Pricing: included in your website (no additional charge)

Landing Page

Think of a landing page as a well-placed billboard along a highway that perks the curiosity of your buyers just enough to have them take the exit and see what you have to offer. Of course all this happens digitally but the function is the same. When a buyer sees your landing page, they read or watch what you have to share, and then choose to leave their email address with you or not.

- Common system: Leadpages.net
- Pricing: Free - $40+ per month

Email system

This is not your email inbox. This is email marketing and it is how you stay connected to people interested in learning more about your PB&J. For instance when we released this book we had a landing page that provided a place for interested people to enter their name and email address before the book was available. When the book was ready we used New Kajabi and sent a bulk email out to those people who had provided their contact information.

- Common system: New Kajabi, Mailchimp, Convert Kit, Aweber, Ontraport, Infusionsoft
- Pricing: Free -- $10+ per month

Products

Your digital products are the PB&J sandwiches that you make. These products can be one-page PDF downloads, year long courses, or even services you provide. The beauty is PB&J is delivered digitally allowing you to leverage your time, money, and effort. You can make a PB&J with practically anything: text, video, audio, and any combination of those.

- Common system: Text: Word, Pages, Evernote, Dropbox; Video: YouTube, Vimeo, Wistia; Audio: Rev.com, Soundcloud. Email, website
- Pricing: Free+

Sales Pages

Your sales page is often a landing page that is written to sell v. inform and educate people. This is where you place the details about your PB&J.

- Common system: Leadpages.net
- Pricing: Average $40 per month (also used as landing pages)

Payment processing

You have to have a way to collect money and will need to set up a payment processor.

- Common system: PayPal, Stripe
- Pricing: Average 2.9% (product purchase price) + 30 cents per transaction

Coupon codes

Who doesn't love a good coupon? Be honest, you're typing "[product name] coupon" before you buy anything online -- we do too! When you're selling your PB&J there may be times that you want to offer different incentives and to do that you will need a way to offer coupon codes.

- Common system: Depends on what you've chosen for your website platform, theme, etc.
- Pricing: Free - $60 per month

Affiliate marketing

When you tell your best-friend about a great restaurant and then he or she goes there wouldn't it be great if the restaurant sent you a check for thirty percent of what he or she spent? Oh yeah! Well that is affiliate marketing in a nutshell. The beauty of the Internet is that it is easy to automatically track where each customer and sale comes from and so businesses without charging anymore for their products and or services can share the sale with the original customer that recommended them.

It's a beautiful win-win situation! Most often the person recommending a business they love will also provide you with additional bonuses as their way of saying "thank you" for using their affiliate link.

As you begin selling your PB&J, you may want to add the functionality of affiliate (*recommending*) marketing to your business model. For example we are affiliates for New Kajabi so when people purchase through our referral link not only do we receive a percentage of the sale from Kajabi but our friends that we are referring also receive a discount not available to the general marketplace. We also have Vacationing Life members that are affiliates for our programs. As they help us expand our reach we are able to help even more families realize they have a PB&J they could make and we are able to share a percentage of each of those sales with them.

To read our Kajabi story – bit.ly/hortonslovekajabi

Affiliate marketing is really a beautiful circulation of a "thank you" economy.

- Common system: New Kajabi. *When looking at other affiliate systems please do your research, unfortunately I (Tamsen) handle severe legal issues when it comes to affiliate marketing and the platforms businesses use. I can't provide a recommendation in this category.*

- Pricing: Free (because it's included in your platform e.g. New Kajabi) - a percentage of the purchase price + a flat fee

There you have it. A list of the essential tools needed to sell your PB&J online.

We included this so you'd know what goes on behind the scenes and are armed with the information you need when you are ready to start selling your PB&J to the world. But *please at this point in time - stay focused on making your PB&J.*

We'd love to help you and that's why we created Vacationing Life Community. We want you to make your PB&J and get it out into the world ASAP!

Acknowledgements

Our words exist because of the inspirational life of Robert Keith Marshall ("Bo", Tamsen's only cousin). Bo lived a life far beyond his twenty-four years and his tragic death forever propelled us into a mindset to squeeze every single little moment out of our days and live BIG like Bo! Bo, we love you more than words. Every word, idea, and thought surrounding "Vacationing Life" is because of you. Thank you for giving all you had, including your life, to protect the safety and security of our family and thousands worldwide. You are the hero of our hearts and a true unsung national hero.

Our beautiful boys, Kip and Tad, you've brought more joy into our lives than we ever thought possible. Everyday you help us see the world for the amazing wonder and playground it is. We treasure watching what you create each and every single day. May you always see and know the value of your PB&J and have the excitement to share it with the world. Create your space, keep moving, and embrace living -- this is what we hope is always true for you.

Aunt Pat and Uncle Mike (Bo's mom and dad), you are the finest examples of unconditional love and encouragement the world has ever known. We are thankful beyond words for the wisdom of the Universe in placing you in our lives. Thank you for bringing Bo into our world, for making so many ideal days possible: Aquamare, Vail, playing in Princeton and NYC, parks, museums, and so many more. You've expanded our eyes, hearts and minds and done so with unconditional love. We love you to the moon and back.

"Mom and dad" "grandma and grandpa" "best in-laws ever!" you are two of our most favorite people and your relentless drive to make so many people's lives better is inspirational. We love you more than words and couldn't do a quarter of what we do without you! Thank you for loving us, the boys, and making so many of our days so fun! Thank you for crafting so we could get these words out onto paper and out into the world. And most of all for being such an amazing example of "cruise while you can!"

Kenny, Travis, and the entire Kajabi family your vision to "enable people to make a living from their hobby or passion" *has truly changed our lives forever.* Knowing that Kip and Tad (baby "Kaj") will grow up knowing how to take what they are excited about and and monetize it in alignment of WHO they are as people is a "thank you" we can't say often enough. In our home Kajabi is a noun, an adverb, and an adjective. You helped us create the legacy we truly wanted for our family. You're not an application or a platform. You're an amazing team of individuals who use their hearts and minds to forever change the trajectory of families. You gave us back our jelly beans!

For all our friends, students, and "vacationing life family members" that make living our #vacationinglife so much fun. We love you all and are thankful beyond words to have our lives woven together with yours.

About the Authors

Tamsen and Chris Horton, creators of the PB&J Course Design™ system are parents passionate about equipping families to share what they know and make money doing it. They know first-hand how to leverage their professional knowledge into multiple income streams all while balancing the demands of two small children and all that life brings with it.

In 2014, after the unexpected and tragic death of Tamsen's beloved and only cousin, Bo, Chris and Tamsen decided to take the location-independent law business Tamsen had into a different realm. With one early-morning phone call, they saw how short life is and didn't want to miss one moment of life together as a family. What started as a term used only between the two of them—"Vacationing Life" quickly became the idea for a movement that would help families all over the world share what they know and make money doing it. Ultimately, allowing families to gain freedom and control over HOW they lived each day.

Now they spend their days doing what they love, surrounded by people that matter to them, and are committed to helping one thousand families also find the life-independence and fun that makes up their life with Kip and Tad.

They love nothing more than taking a nugget of an idea from a member of their community and creating multiple workable and income producing solutions. You can find them most often playing in the sand with their sons and they truly hope that with the ideas and inspiration found within *Easy As PB&J* that you and your family will be able to join them very soon!

Thank You

Thanks so much for reading. It's been our sheer joy to write this book, and we hope you've enjoyed learning the PB&J Course Design system. You now know what to do to share what you know and make money doing it. You have a PB&J inside you!

We've created the PB&J multimedia experience, jam-packed with step-by-step resources to help you with creating your PB&J to share with the world.

To access the multimedia experience –
bit.ly/pbjmultimedia Inside you'll find more stories and examples, videos, and worksheets to help make your PB&J experience even more impactful and enjoyable.

Invite Tamsen & Chris to Your Event
We truly enjoy sharing the both the PB&J and Vacationing Life messages and welcome any inquiries. Please complete this form and we will happily be in touch! bit.ly/vacationinglifeevents

FUNdraising
Interested in our FUNdraising details surrounding this book and our upcoming titles, please complete this form and we will send you the details. bit.ly/vacationinglifefundraising

Institutional Licenses

Are you a teacher, administrator, professional organization or excited parent who would like to see your school, college, university, or company have access to the PB&J ideas. We do offer programs and are happy to share those details with you. All you need to do is complete this form. bit.ly/pbjenterprise

36042384R00102